FARM-RAISED
KIDS

Parenting Strategies for Balancing Family Life with Running a Small Farm or Homestead

KATIE KULLA

foreword by LYNN BYCZYNSKI

Storey Publishing

The mission of Storey Publishing is to serve our customers by publishing practical information that encourages personal independence in harmony with the environment.

Edited by Carleen Madigan and Lisa H. Hiley
Art direction by Erin Dawson
Book design by Alissa Faden

Cover photography by © Janet Moscarello Photography, front, b.; Mars Vilaubi © Storey Publishing, front, t.l.; © Shawn Linehan, front, t.c. & t.r., back

Interior photography by © Katie Kulla, 2, 4, 12, 14, 16 r., 18 m.r., 30, 31 m.r., 35, 37, 40, 48 b.c., r., & t.c., 49 b.c., b.r., t.r., 55 b.r., l. & t.r., 59, 64, 68 b.l., 71 l.m., 76, 84, 87, 98, 99, 120, 135, 147, 157 t.l. & l.m., 204, 209, 213, 214, 216, 218, 220 t.; © Shawn Linehan, vi, 6, 9 t.l., b. & m.r., 10 b. & t.r., 17, 18 b.l. & t.r., 21 all but b.r., 24, 25, 28, 31 all but m.r., 34, 39, 43, 46, 48 t.l. & b.l., 49 t.m., 50, 55 b.c. & t.c., 56, 62, 68 r. & t.l., 71 t. & b.l., 72, 75, 82, 91, 93, 96, 101, 102, 110, 112 b., 114, 122, 150, 154, 157 b., 159, 160, 163, 166, 168, 170, 174, 184, 188, 190, 193, 200, 202, 219 r., 226

Additional photography by © Alyson Larkin and Andrew Larkin, iv, v, 18 t.l., 21 b.r., 26, 54, 112 t.l., 129, 149, 157 r.m., 185, 196, 220 b.; © Christine Anderson and Cast Iron Farm, 126; courtesy of Corinne Hansch, 10 t.l., 18 b.r., 88; Courtesy of Daisy Remington, 16 l., 92, 180, 183, 221; © Eyva Tunku Anor, 69 r., 89; photo by Finn Hopper, courtesy of Sarah Finger, 207; Courtesy of Ian MacLellan, 116; © Janet Moscarello Photography, 112 t.r., 119, 144; © Kendra Knaggs Photography, 23, 106, 109, 121, 130, 142, 171, 178; © Kristin Pool Cohen, 9 t.r., 53, 219 l.; Mars Vilaubi © Storey Publishing, 69 c., 71 b.r., 140, 152, 157 t.r.; © Noëlle Westcott Photography, 143, 161, 172; Courtesy of Raven Berman, 198, 199, 211

Illustrations by Katie Kulla

Text © 2024 by Katherine Kulla
© Storey Publishing/Foreword by Lynn Byczynski

Storey Publishing
210 MASS MoCA Way
North Adams, MA 01247
storey.com

Storey Publishing is an imprint of Workman Publishing, a division of Hachette Book Group, Inc., 1290 Avenue of the Americas, New York, NY 10104. The Storey Publishing name and logo are registered trademarks of Hachette Book Group, Inc.

ISBNs: 978-1-63586-671-1 (paperback);
978-1-63586-761-9 (ebook)

Printed in China by Toppan Leefung Printing Ltd. on paper from responsible sources
10 9 8 7 6 5 4 3 2 1

TLF

Library of Congress Cataloging-in-Publication Data on file

For all the parents, grandparents, aunties,
uncles, teachers, mentors, nannies, and
babysitters who invest time, care, and love
in raising our future generations

CONTENTS

PART 2: AGES AND STAGES IN THE FARM FAMILY

FOREWORD

I met Katie Kulla in 2007, when I was publishing *Growing for Market* magazine and she proposed an article advising small farmers to start a blog. At the time, that was an innovative idea—so much so that Katie had to define "blog" in the first paragraph.

I said yes, the article appeared in the magazine, and thus began a long-running relationship, with Katie writing at least once a year about some new thing she and Casey were doing on their farm in Oregon. Over the years, she introduced *GFM* readers to many cutting-edge ideas, practices, and tools. Through her writing, I came to know her as an especially thoughtful person. The word that comes to mind as I look back on how she built her farm and career is *intentional*. She has always been good at articulating goals and then acting in ways to reach them.

So I wasn't surprised to learn that Katie is also intentional about parenting. Like a talented primary-school teacher, she thinks about what children need to be happy and well adjusted, and she creates opportunities to lead them in that direction. I am often delighted by the glimpses of her family life I get from her social media—wilderness vacations, family Wordle competitions, art projects. Her children seem joyful and creative.

Of course, a farm is the best possible place to raise children, in my opinion. That was one of the main reasons my husband and I started farming in 1988. We knew we wanted children, and we wanted to stay home with them. We wanted to create a place of peace and beauty in which to raise them. We hoped to re-create my husband's idyllic childhood growing up on a farm in western Nebraska in the 1950s and '60s. So we left our city jobs, mine as a newspaper reporter and his as a nonprofit administrator, and started an organic vegetable and flower farm.

Looking back, I think we were largely successful. The path wasn't smooth, and it didn't go exactly as planned, but we managed to farm and raise two kind, capable children, now in their 30s. Neither has chosen to farm (yet!), but both feel that farming gave them a valuable set of skills and experiences.

"One of the things I appreciate most about growing up on the farm is the independence it gave us as kids, and the amount of time we spent outside," our son, Will, said. "Maybe it's just the difference in the available technology, or maybe it's due to living in town now, but I always felt like there were so many more ways to entertain ourselves outside back then. We had to really use our imagination all day every day!"

Our daughter, Laurel, also emphasized the value of a childhood spent mostly outdoors. "I learned to do physical work, which helped me when I got a job on an archaeological dig. And I gained an ecological perspective that my peers didn't necessarily have."

On our 20-acre farm, our kids had the run of fields, barns, treehouses, ponds, and a stream. They absorbed knowledge about plants, animals, weather, and natural systems. They were not afraid of insects or snakes or other fellow creatures, although they did learn when to keep their distance. They were fit, active children who stayed busy, making up games in the barn or curling up with a book while we worked nearby. As they grew into adolescence, they were assigned work—real work, important to the farm's bottom line. And they earned money as well as self-respect from working. When they were old enough to drive, they made deliveries, and they paid for a share of college tuition by growing and selling cherry tomatoes.

They also learned about people, because farms like ours and those featured in this book are not insular. They are beehives of activity and interactions with customers, vendors, employees, school groups, garden clubs, and so on.

Every generation of parents has something to contend with. As much as I use and appreciate technology, I feel lucky that I was able to raise my children before it became prevalent. Working together on our farm, we were able to buffer our kids from a frenetic and consumerist culture. Today, the larger world is right there in our pockets, pinging and beeping at us wherever we go. This book will help with the challenges of farming and parenting today.

I enjoyed learning about how Katie and Casey and many other parents have been navigating today's parenting culture. I expect *Farm-Raised Kids* will be of keen interest to everyone who has a farm and wants children, or to those who already have children and are considering farming. In either case, I say: Go for it! Farming is a beautiful way to raise a family.

—LYNN BYCZYNSKI, founder of *Growing for Market* magazine and author of *The Flower Farmer, Market Farming Success,* and *The Vegetable Garden Planner*

LIFE ON OUR FARM

In December 2009, a record cold snap hit our Oregon farm. My husband, Casey, put chains on our box truck and we drove to our final vegetable delivery of the year. Though the roads were icy, we wanted to make sure our customers got the last of the harvest before we took a winter break. Many of our farm members came to vegetable pickup bearing end-of-season gifts, which this year also included baby quilts and knitted booties. We chatted about holiday plans and my due date (which had just passed). I rode home with my arms resting around the bulk of my belly, feeling our baby wake up and stir as the truck bumped us along.

Two days later, I pulled a jacket over my pajamas, put on boots, and headed outside into freezing weather with Casey to walk laps around our vegetable fields. We walked past row-covered Brussels sprouts and cabbage, but for once our thoughts weren't on what might survive the cold. Instead, we were focused on my breathing and the progress of this natural miracle. Casey supported me when contractions forced me to pause, and soon we were back inside our cozy farmhouse, where I labored through the dark evening, in front of a fire, our farm cats joining our midwives and Casey at my side.

Just past midnight, when all was still and frozen on the farm, our first child was born. Our life and farm were never the same again.

The days after Rusty's birth are a blur, as they are for many parents!

WHY I WROTE THIS BOOK

Casey and I had been farming for six years before Rusty was born—two in training and four operating our own farm. At that point, we felt confident in our ability to farm. We knew what challenges to expect and had resources for ideas and help when we needed it. But we really didn't know what to expect when we became parents or how that new important role in our life would affect our existing role as farmers. Suddenly we were responsible for not only feeding hundreds of people in our community but also being loving parents to our son.

Farming is a unique occupation in that many people expect to be able to do it *at the same time* as physically being with children. We have this image of a "family farm" promoted to us through nostalgic historical literature, as well as through modern social media feeds full of images of parents and children all working happily together on the farm.

The reality of balancing these responsibilities can be complicated in our contemporary world, where we have different parenting styles and expectations than in previous generations. Often households need (and want) more than one parent working (sometimes both on and off the farm). Childcare can be difficult to find (or afford) in rural areas. Even in farming and homesteading families where one parent focuses on being the primary caregiver, that parent is often still actively involved in daily operations or chores that require a constant balancing of priorities and navigating safety concerns for children.

WE NEED FARMS AND FARMERS

These struggles are real, and they have big implications for our communities as the average age of farmers increases and the number of farmers decreases. In the United States, where I live, there is growing concern about the future of agriculture and food security.

Shoshanah Inwood is a former farmer who is now a rural sociologist and associate professor at Ohio State University. Much of her research focuses on social factors that affect farm growth, especially the barriers and challenges for younger farmers and their families. As Shoshanah pointed out to me, young farmers can face significant overlap in their life purposes. "We want farmers when they're young and have strong backs, but that time overlaps with when they're having children," she explained. "How does this very vulnerable point in your life course affect your farm trajectory?"

To ensure future generations of farmers and healthy stewardship of the land, we need to be talking about how to help today's farmers and homesteaders navigate the many challenges they face, including balancing their farm work and family life. I hope *Farm-Raised Kids* will be one piece of that puzzle, a way to provide inspiration and connect farmers in many communities to ideas and solutions and resources.

As I wrote this book, I remembered my former self—that young farmer who sat looking into her baby's face and pondering how it would all work out. How would Casey and I navigate the joy of meaningful work in the fields and the joy of raising our child? I would have loved to read a book like this while I sat and nursed, full of questions about the future of our farm business and the future of our family.

FOR YOU, DEAR READER

As I write these words, I find myself wondering who *you* are and why you've picked up this book at this point in your life.

Are you a seasoned farmer who's just found out you are expecting your first child? Do you already have kids and now you are pondering a big lifestyle change from town to rural living? Do you have a giant urban garden that you work in on weekends with your kids or use as the basis for homeschool lessons? Are you a farmer-employer who wants to relate better to your employees who have children?

I wrote *Farm-Raised Kids* for all of you. The scale, location, family dynamics, and goals can all vary, but I wrote this book for anyone who is involved in growing crops or raising livestock and is also parenting (or has employees who parent) children. To me, these are two of the most important tasks in our society—the most fundamental work. Farmers and homesteaders steward the land and grow food for us. Parents (and other primary caregivers) help young humans grow into loving, capable, responsible adults. Both roles involve significant and ongoing daily work: sowing seeds, changing diapers, watering animals, making family meals, weeding, driving kids to school, managing employees, sitting up with sick kids in the night in the house, sitting up with lambing ewes in the night in the barn.... It's a lot.

OUR FARMING-PARENTING STORY

Of course, we (and our farm) survived our own transition, and Casey and I went on to have our daughter, Dottie, not quite three years later. The intervening years have been filled with joy and growth and constant evolution. Part of why I am writing this book for people coming from many different angles of farming/homesteading and parenting is because, over the years, Casey and I have been in different places ourselves.

Our kids have always helped us with farm chores, such as bunching green onions for our CSA.

We started our farm, Oakhill Organics, in 2006 on one acre of rented land outside McMinnville, Oregon. At the time, we were young—only 25 and 26—and filled with energy and enthusiasm. We were able to use savings to help build our farm business, and both of us worked full-time on the farm from the beginning. We grew organic vegetables for farmers' markets and for our CSA (Community Supported Agriculture) program. The next winter, we were able to buy a bigger parcel of land where we built a very small house, putting down our permanent farm roots on Grand Island, an island in Oregon's Willamette River.

We decided to start a family three years later, and that's when we hired our first employees. It was quite the year of growth: managing people, growing a baby, preparing to be parents. After our son was born, I stepped back from doing as much physical labor on the farm for a while and we hired more help, which all represented big changes in my life and for our farm's operation and budget.

Three years later we went through another growth period when we had our second child, expanded our acreage, and added many new enterprises to our farm, including livestock. For two years we operated a "full diet" style of CSA, aiming to provide our customers with most of their food. We eventually transitioned to a less intensive model, phasing out our livestock after a few more years to return to our vegetable-and-fruit origins. We continued to experiment with our farm's scale, and eventually we settled at a small size that we could once again run with only our own labor.

In this time our children grew, and as I'll talk about throughout the book, our childcare strategies shifted depending on their needs, the work of the farm, and what was available. When they got to school age, I started doing more formal lessons at home, and as of the writing of this book, we still homeschool our now 10- and 13-year-old children.

But our farm has gone through more big changes in recent years. After 15 years of operating our CSA, we decided to pause our commercial farming activities at the end of 2020. Casey and I had both discovered other work we wanted to pursue, and we were ready for a sabbatical from the intensity of farming and growing food for others. And so we began a new stage of our family's life as homesteaders with off-farm income. We still live on our farm,

Dottie and Rusty have grown to be full members of our farm team, not just our family.

and we grow all our own fruits and vegetables and sell some at a local market. But there are other parts to our life now, too, and the rhythm of our weeks has shifted as farming has become our "after-hours" occupation rather than our primary job. Our kids are older and more capable now, too, adding a new element to their involvement in every season.

A DIVERSITY OF STORIES

An important lesson I've learned through all these evolutions is that there's no right way to do any of this, and all of it can be fulfilling. I hope that our variety of experiences can provide insight into the many possible paths a farmer or family might take toward their own goals.

But my experiences are still limited to my own life, so for this book I reached out to other farmers and homesteaders to hear their stories and insights. In every chapter you'll hear not just my voice but also the voices of other parents and caregivers who have faced variations on similar problems and come up with unique solutions. I interviewed a wide variety of farmers to be able to offer you a diversity of perspectives from people growing in different regions, with different family dynamics and business models, and including both homesteaders and larger-scale commercial growers.

Again, the unifying thread is that all these people are caring for children while also growing crops and/or raising livestock. They are profoundly invested in nurturing both the land and future generations. As, I imagine, are you.

May this book be a tool for helping you, your family, and your farm thrive. Ultimately what is most powerful are the solutions and ideas that *you* devise. To that end I've included discussion questions at the close of each chapter— these are intended for you to use in having conversations with your partner/ family or for journaling. Consider reaching out to other farmer-parents and start a reading and discussion group to gain even more insight (and support!) from real people living through similar stages of life and work. I encourage you to avoid judgment of yourself and others when discussing these questions so that you can be honest about your resources, goals, real limitations, and dreams.

As you'll see in this book, combining farming and parenting can be beautiful. And, as you'll see in this book, combining these roles can also be really challenging. Both are true, and I hope this book helps you find solutions when you hit the inevitable challenges on your way to the joyful, beautiful parts.

Katie

WHO'S IN THIS BOOK?

You'll find more information about the farms and homesteads included in this book on pages 218 and 219, but here's a quick snapshot of the families I interviewed.

AVERAGE SIZE OF PROPERTY: 1–30 acres

SMALLEST LAND BASE: Double lot in a city

LARGEST LAND BASE: 1,400 acres

AVERAGE FAMILY STRUCTURE: Two parents and two children

SMALLEST FAMILY: One parent and one child

LARGEST FAMILY: Two parents and ten children

LARGEST FARM COMMUNITY: Five households living on one farm

CROPS PRODUCED: Vegetables, fruit, berries, nuts, meat, eggs, milk, honey, flowers, dry beans, grains, seeds, fiber, and more

LOCATIONS: United States, Canada, New Zealand; rural, suburban, urban

RELATIONSHIP TO THE FARM/HOMESTEAD: Primary operator, co-operator with partner, part owner of cooperative farm, farm employee, resident renter, home/landowner

FAMILY FARMING EXPERIENCE: Multigenerational farm families, first-generation farm families

HOUSEHOLD INCOME: All from farm, partial from farm, none from farm

FAMILY'S LIVING LOCATION: On the farm or homestead, in a home nearby

PART

1

THE
FARM
FAMILY
LIFE-
STYLE

Our family in 2016

WHY MIX
FARMING
AND
CHILDREN?

WHEN I LOOK BACK at photos of our son from his first year of life, almost every one features an element of our farm, too: my husband, Casey, wearing sleeping Rusty in a pouch while taking a field walk; Rusty smiling while teething on fresh green snap peas; Rusty sitting on the floor of our vegetable wash station playing with the gentle spray of a hose during a heat wave; Rusty taking some of his first steps on the soft-packed path of our winter greenhouse.

For Casey and me, the choice to become farmers came before the choice to have children. We had been farming for four years before our first child was born, and so he was born into a farm family. We even gave him a vegetable-inspired name—although he goes by "Rusty," his full name is Russell Sprout (after a vegetable that is in season around his winter birthday). He was marked as a farm kid from birth.

Operating our commercial vegetable farm was much more challenging and difficult after we became parents, for many of the specific reasons you'll hear about in other chapters of this book. I can't speak to how being a farmer might have made parenting more or less difficult, but the combination has certainly felt complicated at times.

But for the most part, Casey and I have been grateful for the opportunity to raise our children in this lifestyle and this setting. And though they also acknowledge the challenges, the many other farmers I connected with for this book express gratitude as well. In the twenty-first century, it feels like an increasingly rare and privileged gift to provide our children a lifestyle with the potential for lots of outdoor time, free play, real work, and abundant access to high-quality food.

While I don't want to gloss over the obstacles and difficulties farmer-parents face, in this chapter I want to make space to deliberately celebrate the best parts—the unique experiences that keep farm families going on the hard days. Many later chapters go deeper into some of these benefits, but you can think of this chapter as an initial pep talk and revisit it on the days when your journey feels rough.

Rusty grew up immersed in the landscape and lifestyle of our farm. Vegetables were his first solid foods, and our fields were his first playground.

A NATURE-RICH EXPERIENCE

Several of the farmers I interviewed mentioned the same book, *Last Child in the Woods: Saving Our Children from Nature-Deficit Disorder*. I read this book well before we had our children. In it, journalist Richard Louv documents the profound recent changes in how kids play and interact with the outdoor world. He contrasts his own childhood, filled with free play outside, with that of his children, which involved many more structured indoor activities.

Louv and the people he cites and interviews see this lack of outdoor time as a fundamental problem for children (and all of us), and he coined the phrase "nature-deficit disorder" to describe the slew of negative effects that come with a more sedentary, less imaginative, indoor-based lifestyle. For individuals, Louv sees a cost in the decrease in physical and mental health as well as the ability to focus and think creatively. For society, Louv worries that raising generations of children without intimacy with the natural world will reduce the number of voices that can speak with love in defense of the environment and preserving our landscapes—or the number of people who even value the land and the natural world at all.

Louv then shares examples of how we can reverse the trend as a society and as individual families by prioritizing outdoor play spaces and encouraging more open-ended play and exploration.

For many farm families, the farm itself is the solution to nature-deficit disorder. Children on farms can live, play, and work

> **The BEST thing about family farming is...**
>
> *My children have this inherent connection to the earth but also to growing food. And everybody they know in their community is doing that and is involved with that. It's pretty magical.*
>
> **BROOKE BRIDGES, SOUL FIRE FARM**

Farms and homesteads can provide children with fun and inviting landscapes for learning about the natural world right outside their door.

immersed in outdoor settings and natural processes in a way that is unprecedented for most children today.

John McCafferty and his partner are raising three children at Pleasant River Produce in New Zealand. He said that his oldest, now 11, has had "nature knowledge" her entire life. "She's got this amazing seasonal awareness that I didn't develop until my 20s," he said. "From a very young age, she also developed great plant identification skills." He said that he taught her how to use some of the plants in his garden as soon as she could pay attention. "Even before she was speaking, she was able to find dock to deal with the little nettle sting she had on her foot."

Amy Frye and her husband are raising their two children at their vegetable farm, Boldly Grown Farm, in Washington State. Until recently they were commuting to their farm, and it's new for them to live on the farm itself and spend more time there, yet her children already know about farming and food. "Our son loves pulling a carrot out of the ground," she said about her six-year-old. "At dinner last week he asked, 'Why do we farm organic instead of not organic?' And I was like, 'How do you even know to ask that question? That's amazing.' There are subtle ways we're not even seeing that our children are absorbing knowledge and understanding."

Benina Montes and her husband are raising their four children (ages 6 to 12) at their 1,200-acre farm in California. She said they already have a grasp on the bigger picture of food systems and where life comes from. "They understand there's a ram and a ewe, and when we put them out together, we get babies," she said. She said they've also witnessed loss and understand the circle of life; growing up with the animals and the land has given them awareness of how it's all connected. "I feel like they have empathy and appreciate where their food comes from and how we all have to protect everything," she said. "Because this is where we live. We don't want to poison it. We want to treat everything well, make it better than how we found it."

"My children have seen a gazillion babies born, so they're not creeped out by it."

—BENINA MONTES

OUTDOOR LIVING

Kids on farms and homesteads can explore, move, play, and work using all their senses in their outdoor environments. Even just walking on different natural surfaces, such as mud or dry grass, creates opportunities for them to experience new sensations.

ROOM TO RUN

With access to time and space spent outdoors also naturally comes lots of physical movement. In *Grow Wild: The Whole-Child, Whole-Family Nature-Rich Guide to Moving More*, biomechanist Katy Bowman writes about how modern environments have eliminated most of the organic, everyday movement from people's lives, including for children. Where food procurement once required walking, squatting, bending, and leaning, today very few people are involved in any part of their food production or gathering. Our lives are shaped by the "convenience" of *not* moving. As a result, Bowman says, we are a "super-sedentary culture." She makes the case that movement is an important part of being physically healthy—and not just movement in short-duration contexts such as exercise classes. Bowman proposes that we really should be moving all day, and that kids especially need to be moving to flourish and grow healthy bodies.

A farm lifestyle provides families an alternative to a stationary lifestyle of convenience and screens. Farm kids use screens, too, but with access to open outdoor spaces, there are plentiful opportunities for big-movement play and for engaging in meaningful and movement-filled chores and work. Farm kids move all day long: walking to the barn to feed animals in the morning, playing outside with siblings, climbing trees, digging in gardens, swinging on rope swings, riding bikes around the fields, taking food scraps to the pigs after dinner—almost every form of play or work on the farm gets kids outside and moving in organic ways.

LOTS OF GOOD FOOD

Farm kids also have access to plentiful, good, nutritious food. At age 10 and 13, my children are only just now beginning to understand what a gift it is to have easy, abundant supplies of year-round fruits and vegetables growing right outside our door. On summer days they walk out to snack in the orchard or berry patches. When Casey or I harvest for dinner, we carry in armloads of vegetables that we lay out on the large wooden counter in our kitchen: piles of kale, heads of cabbage, stacks of red peppers, a mound of onions. That sight never fails to bring me deep joy and a sense of security, and it is a reality our children have grown up with. Even though many farmers (us included) may make less income than what might be possible in other jobs, there is a feeling of richness in having as many vegetables as your family can eat (or eggs or fresh milk or flower bouquets on display).

That immersion in farm-fresh food often leads to kids who eat vegetables and enjoy a diversity of flavors and textures. I can't guarantee this, and our kids have both gone through picky stages at times, but overall I've watched farm kids grow up to have a wonderful appreciation for food. At the same time, they're naturally getting all the benefits of a diet high in nutrients, fiber, and all the other healthy things that have a big impact on our physical and mental health.

A SHARED FAMILY PURPOSE

Another benefit for most families is the ability to spend time together and have shared work, especially as children grow older and can help support the work of the farm. Farming is one of the very few occupations in which we expect parents to work with their children present, either on the same land or even in the same space. Logistically, this expectation can be hard to live up to during the earliest years of parenting. But when families live where they farm, children inevitably get to observe and participate in their parents' work in a way that's rare for most families. Even farmers who don't live on the farm often share their work with their children through the produce they bring home, and by taking them to the farm to do chores or enjoy the outdoor

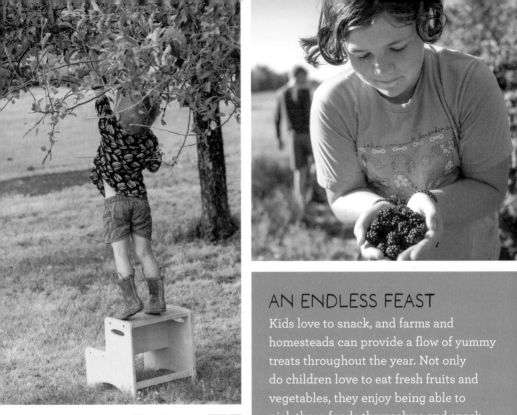

AN ENDLESS FEAST

Kids love to snack, and farms and homesteads can provide a flow of yummy treats throughout the year. Not only do children love to eat fresh fruits and vegetables, they enjoy being able to pick these foods themselves and snack whenever they want.

SOME STATISTICS

On a farm or homestead, safety for kids should be a priority for parents, as it's a legitimate concern. According to a 2022 bulletin from the National Children's Center for Rural and Agricultural Health and Safety (NCCRAHS), 7,469 children suffered injuries on farms in 2014, and this number is considered a low estimate because of underreporting (the 2014 data is the most recent I could find when writing in 2023). In other words, about 33 children are injured in farm-related incidents every day. Most of these injuries are related to the farm environment rather than directly to doing work.

More sobering: On average, a child dies on a farm in the United States every three days—a statistic representing profoundly tragic losses for individual families. The two biggest risks to children on farms are equipment (especially tractors, ATVs, and vehicles) and large animals.

For excellent resources about kids and farm safety, visit Cultivate Safety, a website run by the NCCRAHS. (See Suggested Reading and Other Resources, page 222.)

spaces. And, of course, for homesteading families, the work of growing food and raising animals is often very much a shared purpose that fills nonwork hours and weekends.

Feeling like they can contribute to their parents' endeavors can be very empowering for children and give them a sense of belonging to something much bigger than themselves. Amy Frye of Boldly Grown Farm said she already sees this sense of proud ownership in her two-year-old daughter. "I ask, 'Where's this carrot from?' And my daughter says, '*My farm!*' It's pretty cute," Amy said. "She doesn't even say 'your farm,' it's '*my* farm.'"

Katrina McQuail grew up at Meeting Place Organic Farm in Ontario and returned as an adult to join her parents in the work and eventually buy the farming business outright. "When I was younger, I thought, 'There's no way I'm going back.' Yet, here I am," she said. The thought of someday having children was part of what compelled Katrina to return. She and her husband are now raising their three children at the farm.

Katrina's father holding her newborn son, Hustis

"*As I was thinking about becoming a parent, I was attracted to coming back to the farm. It was an incredible childhood. My sister and I roamed the farm, and we spent a lot of time with my dad because he was the primary farmer. Now my children are having the same experience.*"

—KATRINA McQUAIL

As Katrina's experiences show, multigenerational farms can offer the opportunity for grandchildren and grandparents to work and play together daily. Many other farm families have extended family or friends join them in living on or near their land, expanding the sense of shared purpose to a small community of people who chip in in different ways. For example, grandparents might help with childcare of younger children while older children are doing the daily animal chores, and a friend living on-site might help make deliveries.

For parents, farms and homesteads themselves can also be a way to build assets and businesses to benefit their children later. Bil Thorn and Kate Harwell of Sky Island Farm in Washington said that they have made all their farming choices with their kids in mind. "We built this farm business for the kids—so that we can be home with the kids," said Bil.

"With the farm, our kids can have a business to run later if they want. Or we can potentially sell the business later and have something to leave for them." —BIL THORN

Benina Montes and her siblings grew up on their family's farm and now operate individual farming enterprises, with their parents still nearby.

A SENSE OF COMMUNITY

Children in these extended farm-family networks can grow up with a strong sense of how their efforts contribute to something larger than themselves, but farms can build this feeling even beyond the family unit. Emily Board and Dan Brisebois are two of the 10 owners of Tourne-Sol Cooperative Farm in Quebec. They don't live on-site or have their children present while they're working, but the co-owners have found ways to incorporate their families into farm life through monthly barbecues at the farm.

"That's when all the kids can get together," said Emily. "They're just this giant herd of children, and they roam around the farm as a big team.... Because we have these social points at the farm, the kids do see what we're doing, and they understand how we fit into a community." Dan said that having so many other parents as co-owners of their farm has also helped them have a built-in support network of families with similar values. "It makes our lifestyle feel normal to our kids. They can see a lot of other people living it."

> *"My kids have space to just be themselves and freedom to explore different ways of being out in the green spaces."*
>
> **—ALYSON LARKIN**

Alyson Larkin and her husband, Andrew, have found a similar support network while raising their three children at Wingspan Farm in Oregon. They rent one of three homes on this property, and all three of the families in residence share the work of tending the large garden, taking care of animals, and planting native trees in the forest. Being part of a larger farm community has helped her children embrace the work. "Even if at first they feel like they don't want to do this," she noted, "they always end up having fun, and they always enjoy their time within community."

BUILDING A POSITIVE FUTURE

Seeing the results of their efforts also grows kids' work ethic and their confidence in their abilities. Alyson's children helped their community plant 4,000 trees in one year and then plant hundreds of trees every year since then. Seeing that they can make a difference in their family and on a farm provides an essential lesson in understanding their own agency and responsibility in the world and the future. That awareness can develop from projects and work, such as tree planting or helping do farm chores, and it can also grow just from play. "Being outside builds confidence," Alyson said.

Having a space where they can play and where, eventually, they can contribute in a meaningful way with work also provides children with a positive view of their own future. Later, whether they decide to become farmers themselves or not, kids growing up in a farm family develop employable skills and get a huge head start on their peers in building endurance and resilience for challenging work. These skills can aid them in whatever path they decide to pursue.

Multigenerational farmers Katrina McQuail and Benina Montes both did make the choice to return to their families' farms to help steward them into the future and provide their families' livelihood. Katrina said that growing up on a sustainable farm helped her feel like she was a part of a positive solution for future generations. "Working in nature and farming is part of what gives me hope for the future," she said. "Part of what helped us want to have kids is that hope."

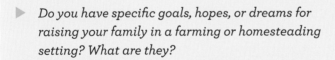

DISCUSSION AND JOURNALING QUESTIONS

▶ *Do you have specific goals, hopes, or dreams for raising your family in a farming or homesteading setting? What are they?*

▶ *What are your inspirations and who are your role models for seeking a farming lifestyle for your family?*

▶ *If you are already farming with children, what parts of that experience bring you the greatest joy?*

CHAPTER

2

PLAY
AND
FUN
ON THE
FARM

ON A FARM, EVERY SAFE NOOK and cranny of the land can be an opportunity for play. Some spaces offer room for transient play—a field to race through on the way to pick peas for a snack—while other places become favorite spots for children to visit regularly as they exercise their imaginations and bodies.

Just beyond the lawn in front of our house, where the ground gently slopes down to the fields, you'll find a square plot of land that has been many things over the years. It's sandier than much of our field and drains quickly in spring, so before we had children, we liked to till and plant there before the rest of our land was ready. But when our children were young, we decided it was the perfect size and location for a garden for them. They got to choose what plants they wanted to grow, and we helped them sow, plant, water, and weed. They grew crops they loved—lots of different kinds of melons, cucumbers, flowers, and even fennel. They harvested entries for the county fair and brought home ribbons to hang on their walls. They played hide-and-seek in the garden with friends and hid "eggs" (large wooden beads) for each other to find in spring.

Dottie and Rusty show off their prizewinning county fair entries.

And then one winter, between seasons, they started digging in the fallow garden. And they kept digging ... and digging ... and digging. Instead of building an aboveground fort, they dug below-grade rooms and channels and alcoves. The holes got so deep that when we had people visiting the farm, we put caution tape around "The Pit" to avoid having them stumble into it after dusk. The kids hauled branches trimmed off our walnut tree and built roofs. They brought out plastic animal toys and situated them in different parts of their landscape. They filled channels with water and watched the water flow into the gopher holes they uncovered. Twice they asked Casey to fill in The Pit with the tractor so they could start over, digging fresh new holes.

This past summer, after it was filled in again, the kids (then 9 and 12) asked Casey if he could use the tractor's front loader to build some bike features: jumps and a banked berm. In the evenings, Casey and the kids now watch tutorials on how to build bike trails, and my 13-year-old son goes out with a shovel and a wheelbarrow and moves earth for hours on end, not only in The Pit but also all over our farm.

All of these manifestations of gardens and pits and bike ramps have been play, on a large scale, that has allowed my children to create, imagine, explore, and grow.

OUTSIDE ENERGY

Outdoor play is a powerful release for challenging kid energy. When they're beginning to misbehave indoors in a way that means they're bored or really need to move their bodies in a big way (which is a genuine need for kids, just like food and sleep), it's wonderful to be able to direct that energy outside.

A FARM IS A GREAT PLACE TO PLAY

In *Last Child in the Woods*, Richard Louv talks about the "criminal-ization of natural play" in public spaces. I've encountered this myself, such as in a beautiful state park where my kids and their friends were admonished to stop climbing a (very climbable!) shore pine tree. It's possible there was concern about the tree's health, but I think safety and liability were also main concerns for the parks department. Likewise, many public spaces discourage visitors from picking up or collecting natural objects like rocks, sticks, leaves, or flowers. It makes sense to avoid having visitors pick up so many natural objects that they might detract from other visitors' experiences or hurt the environment. Even if necessary, such constraints in public and school spaces have cur-tailed much of the kinds of play kids might naturally gravitate toward.

Today, instead of encouraging free exploration, building, collecting, climbing, or digging, public spaces for children are usually designed for prescribed uses: climbing structures, swings, and so on. These are also important ways for children to play and move their bodies, and many farmers build swing sets and play structures near their houses. But the real gift of having access to land is the ability to engage in messy, imag-inative, constructive play: building forts and fairy houses, digging holes, collecting rocks and sticks, watching small animals, and so much more.

If important safety considerations around the workplaces are addressed, farms can be ideal places for kids to play. They offer easy access to all the elements Louv identifies as being important for kid play: the loose parts of nature, space to roam, and—also essential—*time* to engaged in unstructured, unprescribed play. In the final chapter of this book, I share profiles of young adults who grew up on farms. When I interviewed each of these former farm kids, one of the first things they all mentioned was how much they treasured the play opportunities they had growing up. They each had very specific memories of special spaces around the edges of the farms that they transformed into forts or magical kingdoms of their own.

KEEPING PLAY SAFE ON THE FARM

Free play on the farm can be so wonderfully fun! But farms (and homesteads) are worksites, after all, and so it is essential to make sure that kids are safe while playing. Here are some important basic guidelines for play safety. You can find more at the Cultivate Safety website. (See Suggested Reading and Other Resources, page 222.)

Always supervise young and immature children.

Obviously, the level of freedom we give our children depends on their age and maturity. Young toddlers and preschoolers require constant supervision by an adult or older child. Diane Saleh of Halal Pastures in New York has three children, and her youngest are three and four years old. They are both very interested in machinery and farming equipment. "When it's farming season, we stay right on top of them. Someone has to be around them the entire time," she said. "We feed their curiosity, but they cannot be left alone."

Elementary-school children, depending on their maturity, can start to play on their own with adults nearby. In fact, Diane's

10-year-old daughter is mature enough that her parents trust her to watch her younger siblings as they all play outside together.

Gauge each child's maturity and ability to follow through on rules versus the risk posed by the farm. Alyson Larkin's middle child was only two when they moved to Wingspan Farm. "When we first moved here, he was always with an adult," she said. "And then as the kids got older, it was more of an exploration." Alyson and her husband continually assessed what areas were safe for their kids and with what level of supervision. For example, once the children were 10 or 11 years old, they started letting them play in the farm's forest by themselves. When the kids first started to explore this new expansion of their play area, Alyson and her husband gave them walkie-talkies so that everyone could stay in touch.

Create safe, dedicated play spaces.

For young children especially, it can be helpful to both kids and parents to have safe, dedicated play spaces very close to the house or work areas. These are safe spaces that are well equipped for play, with sandboxes, toys, and the like, and with clear physical boundaries. A farm could have one primary play space or several in key spots. Such spaces can help facilitate the period between when a very young child needs constant supervision and when they're ready to play a little more independently with an adult nearby.

Set physical boundaries.

To reiterate what I've said elsewhere in this book, the two biggest risks for serious injury to a child are vehicles (tractors, ATVs, trucks) and large animals. Water bodies also pose a drowning risk. It's important for parents to place boundaries around these risk areas for their children. You'll need to judge what the important boundaries are for your family based on your farm infrastructure and your children.

At Campfire Farms in Oregon, Christina Menchini's sons are young enough that their outdoor play is confined to the area by the house. This keeps them out of the way of the farm's animal production areas, where there are dangers such as electric fences and breeding sows. "Our house is separated from our farm by an easement to the neighbor's house and the road," Christina said. "It helps a lot with safety because the road is a barrier, and they don't go into a field without adults."

Alyson Larkin's children aren't allowed in their barn without an adult present. She and her husband worry about the potential danger of kids climbing in the hay and interacting with the cows and horses.

Keep dangerous objects out of reach.

In addition to thinking about the spaces where a child might play, consider how to store dangerous tools, equipment, and materials so that they don't pose a risk to your children or visiting children.

"Certain tools have to be put away in a safe place," said Diane Saleh. "Last year my son almost set the greenhouse on fire with a torch." A secured shed or storage room can be a good choice for storing potentially dangerous materials. Remove keys from tractors when not in use.

It's especially important to store firearms properly in a gun safe. "We have guns, so they're in a safe, and none of the kids have the code," said Benina Montes. "An adult has to take a firearm out, and then we're with the kids if they're going to do anything with them."

Talk about safety and your expectations.

As farmers were telling me about all the various tools and techniques they use to keep their kids safe on the farm, the one I heard most consistently was continually educating children about the risks on their properties. This was especially important for older children who are given more time and space to roam without direct supervision. Safety talks included reiterating boundaries and the importance of avoiding certain equipment. Most farmers said that they trusted their older kids to make smart choices, especially once rules were in place.

"All the kids on the farm are such great kids, and they've never pushed boundaries," said Alyson Larkin about her own children and those of other families who live at Wingspan Farm. "I think having so much space allows them the freedom they need, but also they understand their own boundaries, too."

GOOD PLAY HABITS = MORE WORK TIME!

Why do farm kids have so much time to play freely? It's often because their parents are busy working! Farm kids may have many periods of time when they might be expected to play on their own, with or without a parent nearby, depending on their maturity level. For these situations, when a parent would ideally like to get a task done rather than facilitate play, it benefits everyone to encourage independent play habits in a child. Playing independently or with siblings or other children comes naturally for many children, but some need to be coaxed to experiment with different types of play. A child who doesn't like playing in a playhouse might love digging in the dirt for hours. Parents can help children experiment by providing different play aids and creating simple play spaces around the home and farm.

Alyson Larkin brings her youngest child with her to work in the shared garden space at Wingspan Farm in Oregon. This past summer, though he was only three, she expected him to play by himself next to her while she and her husband worked. "We set ourselves up for success when we planned to spend a lot of time in the garden. We always brought a basket of his favorite toys, snacks, and water. That allowed us to work, and he could go back and forth between helping us and playing with his own toys," she said. "And then he would naturally start playing with the stuff the earth gives him, too: rocks and sticks."

John McCafferty said that his 11-year-old daughter is also skilled at playing around the farm. "She's very good at entertaining herself," he said. "She creates little arrangements with debris she finds around the garden and helps herself to food." He said that she'll build tiny scenes out of bits of sticks and plant matter. She'll often build little houses with kitchens and areas for washing up and even tiny pretend campfires outside.

ATTENTION SPANS DIFFER

In my experience, how much work time can be gained while a child plays varies greatly based on their age and temperament. When our children were very young, their independent playtime was unpredictable enough that I considered it "extra time" and kept a list of quick chores I could accomplish if/when the children got engaged in a game in the yard. I'd stay nearby and answer emails from chefs or pay bills until the kids needed my attention. But as they grew older, they became more and more independent and were happy to go dig in their pit for hours at a time.

When our children were preschool age and finally playing for longer stretches, but not yet ready to play far away from us, Casey built a portable playhouse that we could pull out to the fields as a home base for the kids while we harvested or weeded. The goal was to give them a place to store their toys and provide shade from sun and protection from rain. They mostly played in the fields around us, but having that portable house helped us all grow comfortable with the idea that they could entertain themselves while we worked.

Our children developed indoor play habits, too, such as drawing, reading, listening to audiobooks, and playing board and card games together. The ability to make their own source of entertainment feels like an important life skill, right up

Our portable playhouse provided a place for our kids to play independently while we worked nearby.

there with the ability to complete chores and work. It takes creativity, ingenuity, and self-knowledge for a child to decide how to fill their own unstructured time. We have intentionally helped them learn what they love to do around the farm and given them space, time, and the safety to explore those activities.

THE QUESTION OF SCREEN TIME

Perhaps one of the more radical parenting decisions I made for our children was to keep their daily life mostly screen-free until they were older. When they were very young, I experimented with letting them watch shows or play online games at times. Many people want to give kids *some* screen time on a regular basis, and I thought I'd try that approach, too.

But their desire to engage with shows and games seemed to overwhelm their interest in playing on their own or with each other. They seemed to grow bored more quickly on days when they watched shows and would immediately think of screens as the answer to their boredom. They seemed more restless and agitated—quite frankly, they were less pleasant to be around! I found that it was simpler and helped us all feel calmer to forgo screens altogether, and my children found myriad other ways to entertain themselves (with my help). We weren't ultra-strict—our children still watched shows or played on tablets occasionally at their grandparents' house—but at home they didn't have that option and instead they played or looked at books.

Eliminating screens for young children is a way in which even families living in a town or urban environment can help encourage young children to engage with nature and free play both outdoors and inside. For more tips on helping build peaceful home rhythms and encouraging free play, I recommend *Heaven on Earth: A Handbook for Parents of Young Children* by Sharifa Oppenheimer.

Christina Menchini's son plays in a wooded area on their farm. Natural elements plus a few toys can inspire the imagination.

Every family needs to experiment and find their own solutions. Many find that a balance with moderate screen use works quite well for everyone! Parents should make choices that are the best for their family. But rest assured, study after study concludes that kids will not miss out by having their earliest years free from screens and in fact may benefit from a low-tech childhood.

Now that my children are older, they seem highly capable of learning technical skills, and screens have become an important part of their communication and learning life. At 10 and 13, they still have limited access, tailored to those specific needs. And, because of all those years with no screens at all, they still gravitate toward other kinds of activity and take initiative to go play outside, read, draw, help on the farm, and more.

5 FUN IDEAS
FOR OPEN-ENDED FARM PLAY

1 Play with nature.

One of the first and favorite sources of play for kids are natural elements themselves. When they were little, my kids played in mud puddles and dusty patches of ground, splashing or just running dust through their fingers. Bring small shovels, toys, and buckets out to the field or garden so kids can dig. Build a sandbox near the house or in a greenhouse. Put out cups, bowls, and pots near a muddy area and call it a "mud kitchen." Give bigger kids full-size shovels and permission to dig really deep holes, such as "The Pit" we had on our farm.

Let kids collect rocks, flowers, sticks, leaves, and other natural treasures to play with or bring into the house to display. Turn on a sprinkler near the house in summer or invite the kids to play in the edges of an irrigated field. In the heat of summer, we've always had some kind of wading pool in our yard for the kids to use (with supervision)—it started with small bins for our littlest babies to splash in and then graduated to a shallow animal trough and finally to a solid pallet tote that's big enough for all of us to dunk into to cool off.

2 Use your imagination.

Any sort of play can be enhanced with toys that encourage imagination. Many children delight in building little worlds and telling stories as they play alone or with other children. Our children had hours of fun collecting natural objects and building scenes for small plastic animals—I'd step out of the house to find them sprawled on their stomachs in the yard, quietly whispering a story to themselves as they moved a plastic dinosaur through a pile of mint leaves and sticks. They also carried buckets of plastic animals out into the fields to play with among the vegetables (and yes, we still unearth the occasional dinosaur toy when we work up ground).

Dolls, superhero figurines, fairies, trucks, and cars can all serve as characters or vehicles in outdoor, nature-based play. One year our children spent several days picking flowers, pulling off the petals, and taping them as elaborate clothing onto their stuffed animals. If you're not okay with indoor toys getting dirty, designate a collection of toys for outside.

3 Kid-built spaces.

Kids *love* to build forts and houses. And they love to do it themselves. Adult-constructed playhouses can have value, too, of course. We built a mobile playhouse that we could pull out into our fields when Casey and I were both working, but our children had infinitely more hours of fun over the years building their own houses and forts (and, of course, The Pit). Invite your children to create spaces by giving them permission to rearrange materials in big ways in certain (safe) spaces.

If they are old enough, you can even provide them with tools for cutting branches or shovels for digging. Working together, all the children at Wingspan Farm built an elaborate space by cutting out a big empty area inside a blackberry hedge. "You could literally stand up. It was huge," Alyson Larkin said. "They built a fort in there. Each kid had their own little area, and they had a bed."

4 Move around!

Kids love opportunities to move their bodies in *big* ways. Some farm families buy play structures to put in safe play spaces so that kids can have access to slides and swings. Others also buy trampolines. We have two rope swings in our large walnut tree, a slackline, and swings in a shed. But on a farm, opportunities for big play extend beyond the yard. There can be trees to climb; space for playing large, organized games with friends; trails for riding bikes; and room to just run or walk in circles.

"My four- and six-year-old sons like to pull anything with wheels," said Sarah Kostyu of K7 Farm in Michigan. "Dollies, wagons, carts. They load up whatever they are pulling with treasures to bring to their fort." She said she tries to find ways her children can apply their love of pulling things to work around their farm—for example, pretending to be a tree company while helping her clean up fallen branches after an ice storm.

Movement and imagination go well together. "When our kids were younger, it was amazing to see what they came up with," said Alyson. "Sometimes they acted like a totally different person all day long. They were on a boat or in a tree, using their imagination to create different spaces throughout the farm."

5 Care for pets and plants.

Kids can also "play" at farming by having their own small garden or pets/animals. While the maintenance of these spaces can sometimes be viewed as early "work," this is a good example of how work and play are ideally two activities on one spectrum. A child with their own garden can have the fun of picking out seeds and the satisfaction of watching things grow, and can learn the necessity of putting in effort to weed and water. Taking care of a pet can provide infinite hours of pure joy for a child while teaching them about responsibility and care.

FAMILY PLAYTIME

Let us not forget that farms can be a wonderful setting for adults and whole families to play as well! Even though farms are often a place of work, for many families they are also a place for recreation, with adults enjoying the easy access to the outdoors in their spare time just as much as the children do. Part of the important goal of a balanced life is making sure we have a relationship with our land beyond the work.

While our family loves to hike and ride bikes off the farm, we also find many ways to be together right here on our land. We host friends for potlucks, which often include making music or playing games in the fields. We have a big collection of regional field guides that we take when we go on walks through the fields to watch birds and animals together. My daughter and I recently set up a trail camera, and we love to watch the resulting videos of nighttime animals that wander through our farm (coyotes, raccoons, skunks, and lots of feral cats). We have fires in our fire ring, roast marshmallows, and tell ghost stories. On cold, clear winter nights, before bed, we lie out in sleeping bags and look at the stars. We let the kids plan elaborate meals and then help them harvest vegetables and cook. My daughter and I pick flowers and make bouquets for the house all summer long.

KEEPING IT CLEAN

Fostering plenty of fun outdoor play can bring its own logistical challenges. True story: We have broken our washing machine three times trying to wash extremely soiled clothing—for example, after the children literally rolled in mud puddles. To embrace all the wonderful and messy elements of kid farm play, it's important to prepare *everyone* in the household for logistical success so that adults don't get frustrated (and hopefully washing machines don't break).

Designate a mud room or porch in your house. Install coat hooks and put out shoe racks and baskets to provide space for everyone's stuff to be stored easily, even by young children. An organized mud room can help children find what they need to go outside and can also help contain the mess . . . for the most part!

Set up a hose for outside washing up. Yes, really. We do this with our children, and they just had to learn to stand the cold water! We also have a laundry sink in our pantry where they can finish washing up. Their ability to take charge of their own cleaning made all of us feel much more relaxed about them getting very, very dirty at times.

Be okay with stained and ripped clothing. In our house, we all have a few sets of "town clothes" that we aim to keep clean. Everything else is fair game for farm levels of wear and tear. When they were young, our children mostly wore hand-me-downs and secondhand clothing so that we could relax about the level of destruction that happened.

In terms of not ruining the washing machine, sometimes clothes are soiled enough that they need to be rinsed out by hand *before* going in the washer. That's a task I ask my children to do, preferably outside. Even with play, there are so many opportunities to learn responsibility for your body, your belongings, and your home!

Elise Bortz and her family don't live on her farm at Elysian Fields Farm in North Carolina, but they often make time to visit during summer to fish in the three-acre pond there. "It never runs out of water and has a lot of fish," she said. Elise admitted that she personally doesn't like to fish, but her family does. "I go because I enjoy being with them," she said. Even though they don't live on the farm and Elise's children don't have daily work and play opportunities there, fishing on the weekends has provided a positive way for the whole family to interact with and value the land.

Having access to open space for play and creation is a gift and privilege for both children and adults. Elise recalled that during the early stages of the COVID-19 pandemic, she invited neighbors from their street in town to share that opportunity. "'You need to just get out,'" she told them. "'You can go up to the farm and go fishing or something.' Some people definitely took us up on that."

DISCUSSION AND JOURNALING QUESTIONS

▶ *What were your favorite games to play when you were a child? What kind of play felt almost magical?*

▶ *Consider your current home or farm setting. Where might you easily integrate a new safe play space for your child(ren)?*

▶ *Are there any dangers on your farm that don't yet have safeguards or boundaries around them? How might you create boundaries?*

▶ *Do you and other adults have fun on your farm? What kinds of activities, games, or projects might be fun for you and your whole family?*

CHAPTER

3

LIVING
THE
SEASONS

SEASONALITY IS THE WATER we farmers and homesteaders swim in. No matter where we live, the seasons bring changes, and those changes shape every part of our lives, from the kind of work we do all day to the food we harvest and eat. On our Oregon farm, we anticipate the seasons well in advance of their arrival—leeks sown in the February greenhouse are planted in June, grown all summer, and finally harvested on a cold December day almost a year later.

On a farm, not only might we observe four distinct seasons of winter, spring, summer, and fall, but we often have other rhythms that shape our year: the start and end of market season, the greenhouse season for sowing starts, apple-picking season, lambing season. The farm-related work seasons shape the nature of our days, sometimes in profound ways.

Acknowledging the magic and wonder of seasonal living can be one of the unique gifts we offer farm-raised kids. With our lives changing so profoundly from month to month, we can highlight for them the special relationships farmers have with the natural world and its cycles.

NOTICE THE SIGNS

Being intentional about seasonal living can be as simple as paying full attention and helping our children to do so, too. In addition to all the usual seasonal work on their New Zealand farm, Daisy Remington and her family make a point to notice the seasonal signs in the natural world around them. "We play a game called kingfisher-spotting, because in spring there are tons of them," Daisy said. "In summer they disappear. And, then as soon as summer starts to turn into autumn, even though it doesn't look like fall yet, the kingfishers return."

They also listen for crickets as a sign of summer's end. "That's one of our biggest ones to watch for, noticing summer turning to autumn," Daisy said. "Maybe I notice it especially because I'm disappointed that summer is ending." Daisy, who was raised in the United States and moved to New Zealand as an adult, was surprised to find that autumn festivals aren't celebrated in her new country the way they are in many northern hemisphere countries. For her, noticing natural signs brings intention into her family's autumn farm life in the way those festivals from her childhood did.

SEASONALITY

For children as well as adults, the experience of seasonality comes through our senses: different sights, sounds, temperatures, colors, smells, and, of course, flavors.

CELEBRATE THE SEASONS

"The days are getting longer. The nights are getting shorter," sang my four-year-old daughter, Dottie, as we crunched across ice one freezing January day. We'd just passed through the winter holiday season, including the solstice itself, which our family marked very simply by making a batch of fir-needle tea and watching the morning brighten while we sipped it. I explained to the children about the tilted axis of the earth and how it creates our seasons and changes day lengths throughout the year. Ever since that quiet morning, Dottie had been celebrating with her own little song, reminding us that even though winter's cold was upon us, warmer days were coming.

In some ways, observing the seasons is very simple for farmers. Certainly, the rhythms of where we live and our type of farm form part of the foundational physical knowledge farm kids develop as they grow up immersed in the cycles of life. And yet we find that adding an extra layer of celebration and awareness to the seasons—such as a cup of fir tea on the winter solstice—can help heighten the joy of living on the land and growing food. The celebrations remind us to be grateful and see the gifts amid the work. On the flip side, being intentional

Our family shares weekly meals with my parents, offering opportunities to enjoy seasonal foods.

about noting the seasonal changes can help us through some of the harder times of the year. We find the unique parts to celebrate, and remember that changes are always on their way.

At K7 Farm in Michigan, Sarah Kostyu and her family of 12 have developed a number of seasonal celebrations based on notable occasions, such as the first maple syrup and the first day the meat birds leave the brooder for the coop. "The new year is traditionally brought in with venison steaks and peach cobbler on New Year's Eve," said Sarah. Her whole family also enjoys making a game out of finding the first ripe tomato every summer.

FOOD AND FESTIVITIES

Marking the changing seasons can be an opportunity for connection, both within a family and with a larger community. Seasonal foods provide a wonderful opportunity to mark the shifts in the year and to gather together.

Our children have always watched the fields and orchards carefully for signs of the next ripe, sweet farm foods, beginning with the first sugar snap peas in our high tunnels in late April and ending with pears in November. In between is a delicious string of fruits and vegetables, from strawberries to carrots to cherries to plums. Each of those firsts is a moment of celebration in our family, as we enjoy eating them ourselves, in our home, before they are ready for us to pick in large enough quantities to share with customers. Being intentional about celebrating these seasons can be as simple as serving the first strawberries in pretty bowls with whipped cream after dinner and making a point to give thanks for these sweet treats, the harbinger of so many more to come.

But over the years, our family has also enjoyed creating bigger community celebrations out of seasonal foods. One year when we were milking cows and had a glut of strawberries, we invited our customers out for a strawberry ice cream open house and made enough ice cream to feed dozens of people.

For many years, we'd host a larger outdoor dinner party for friends and customers at the end of summer, when the tomatoes, peppers, zucchini, and eggplant were at their peak and we had more of them than we could possibly sell. We'd cook a giant batch of ratatouille with our extras, make a salad, buy bread and cheese, and invite everyone out for a "Ratatouille Rendezvous"—our silly name for a simple gathering to celebrate the farm's survival of another growing season and to rejoice in all the late-summer food. We often felt exhausted at this point of the year, but making the time to celebrate with friends helped us remember how amazing this season really is.

Unique seasonal celebrations usually don't compete with existing holidays, and we can make up the traditions ourselves based on our own values and our favorite foods or activities. Some simple farm-based elements can make for memorable gatherings or traditions: potluck meals with seasonal food, campfires, and farm tours or work parties.

(5) EASY IDEAS
FOR CELEBRATING THE SEASONS

1 Eat with intention and gratitude.

Eating food when it is in season is a natural part of growing your own food, and it's simple to savor these special flavors as they come and go. You can add another layer of intention and gratitude to your family meals of seasonal foods by acknowledging what might be new or changing on your plates and by saying thank-you for every meal, such as with a traditional prayer, song, or your own small ritual. Before starting to eat, our family waits until everyone is seated with our food on our plates. Then we raise our plates of food, look at each other, and say thank-you. It helps bring us present to the moment together.

2 Make a nature table.

A "nature table" is a simple idea usually associated with Waldorf education—a table or surface is dedicated as a place where children (and adults!) can bring in collected natural objects to put on display. We've had a nature table in our living room since our children were very little, and its purpose has evolved over the years. At first it was a great place for the kids to unload their pockets at the end of the day, adding to the table any special rocks or sticks they'd collected on their adventures. But now we use it as a space to celebrate the beauty of the season with bouquets and harvest displays.

3 Keep a "firsts" journal or calendar.

A simple way to observe how seasonal trends shift from year to year is with a "firsts" journal or calendar. This is a place where people in a family write down the date of any kind of "firsts" you want to remember each year: the first blooming daffodil, turkey vulture in the sky, ripe tomato, or fall frost. If you use a "perpetual" calendar (a calendar without specific days of the week assigned to the dates), you can write on it for years and compare how trends shift over time.

Kristin Pool Cohen and her daughters gather apples to mix with honey for Rosh Hashanah.

4 Create a seasonal walk tradition.

Choose a natural space on or near your farm to visit at a regular interval—perhaps monthly or on the first day of each season. On your regular walk there, keep your eyes and ears open for the changes in the place. Our family has one walking trail that is particularly special to us here on the river island where we live. Seeing what is happening in that forest helps us contextualize the changes on our farm in the bigger picture of our region and larger natural cycles. These walks are also a very simple and doable way to help us get away from our own fields and find some balance (see Chapter 6 for more on that topic).

5 Remember the traditional holidays.

Amid all the farming and gardening cycles, traditional holidays happen, too, and many of these holidays have their own customs and rituals that are fun to emphasize on a farm with your own seasonal foods. For example, Kristin Pool Cohen's family enjoys the times when they can celebrate Jewish holidays with gardening and seasonal activities. Apples and honey are traditional foods for the Jewish new year, Rosh Hashanah, celebrated in September. "We like to cook a unique variety of apples," Kristin said.

Alyson Larkin's entire family helps with farm work projects.

CELEBRATE WITH A WORK PARTY

Other food and seasonal work occasions make for natural gathering points, too. Potato planting in spring is a great excuse to invite people out to help and then share a potluck. Late summer and fall are full of opportunities to gather apples and press cider, pick out pumpkins, or harvest potatoes. If you have a favorite crop that often produces in abundance, perhaps it can become the opportunity to build a new gathering tradition around a related meal.

Work parties are a big point of seasonal community for Alyson and Andrew Larkin, who live with their three children at Wingspan Farm, a larger property with three homes. The families sharing the property often work together in their two-acre garden and also organize work parties for bigger projects such as winter tree planting and pruning. "It's been so fun to work together ever since our kids were little, and now they really help," Alyson said. "Just being in community is a celebration." The farm's families also gather for a harvest dinner at the end of every summer, where they feature food grown in the garden.

MAKE TIME FOR CRAFTS AND ACTIVITIES

Another way to raise your family's awareness of the seasons is by doing seasonal crafts or activities. I must admit that I rarely have the patience for elaborate crafts or decorations, but books abound with ideas for people who love those kinds of activities, and there are many very simple activities farm families can do to engage kids of all ages. Some of these even double as a form of play—something a child can do while a parent works or does household chores.

Kristin Pool Cohen and her family live with another family in Super House, a shared house on a large city lot in Portland, Oregon. On their large urban homestead, the families' four children have plenty of space to play outside and garden. Helping in the garden is a major seasonal activity for the kids. In spring, the families go together to buy starts for their garden space, and the kids get to pick out items for their own bed.

The parents also like to organize occasional seasonal crafts and other activities. Throughout summer, Kristin works with the kids to make bouquets. "My grandma always made a lot of bouquets," she said, "and I really like using a lot of different interesting objects like

Marko Colby reads *Better Move On, Frog!* with his son.

seedpods. The kids go scavenging for them with me." In fall, the kids go on a leaf walk and do leaf rubbings and simple art. In December, they make wreaths. Younger kids' wreaths are very simple—just found natural objects glued onto a paper wreath—but the concept can expand with complexity as kids grow and develop more dexterity.

CHERISH THE SEASONS WITH BOOKS

Being intentional about learning and observing seasonal changes can support children's growing awareness of their personal experience and how it fits into the context of the wider world, geographically, culturally, and scientifically. For young kids, picture books that illustrate seasonal rhythms are a good place to start. (I've included a list of suggested titles on pages 57–59.)

SEASONAL PICTURE BOOKS

These are some of our family's favorite seasonal books, plus a few newer ones I've discovered in recent years. Many more delightful books exist beyond these titles, of course, but this is a starter list.

Spring

And Then It's Spring by Julie Fogliano, illustrated by Erin E. Stead

■ ● *Bear Wants More* by Karma Wilson, illustrated by Jane Chapman

Busy Spring: Nature Wakes Up by Sean Taylor and Alex Morss, illustrated by Cinyee Chiu

Flower Fairies of the Spring by Cicely Mary Barker

♥ *Flower Garden* by Eve Bunting, illustrated by Kathryn Hewitt

♥ *Goodbye Winter, Hello Spring* by Kenard Pak

Mama, Is It Summer Yet? by Nikki McClure

★ ● *Planting a Rainbow* by Lois Ehlert

■ *Spring* by Gerda Muller

♥ *Who Likes Rain?* by Wong Herbert Yee

Summer

All in a Day by Cynthia Rylant, illustrated by Nikki McClure

● *Bear and Bunny Grow Tomatoes* by Bruce Koscielniak

♥ *Berry Song* by Michaela Goade

★ *Blueberries for Sal* by Robert McCloskey

♥ *Community Soup* by Alma Fullerton

● *Corgiville Fair* by Tasha Tudor

Flower Fairies of the Summer by Cicely Mary Barker

♥ *Green Green: A Community Gardening Story* by Marie Lamba and Baldev Lamba, illustrated by Sonia Sánchez

● *Growing Vegetable Soup* by Lois Ehlert

♥ *The Hike* by Alison Farrell

♥ *How a Seed Grows* by Helene J. Jordan, illustrated by Loretta Krupinski

How Does My Garden Grow? by Gerda Muller

★ ■ *Jamberry* by Bruce Degen

Peter in Blueberry Land by Elsa Beskow

♥ *Rainbow Stew* by Cathryn Falwell

■ *Summer* by Gerda Muller

♥ *Summer Days and Nights* by Wong Herbert Yee

♥ *The Ugly Vegetables* by Grace Lin

Where Do They Go When It Rains? by Gerda Muller

KEY

■ Board books for youngest readers

★ Some of our family's all-time favorites

♥ Books that feature diverse characters or stories

● Books that don't include human depictions

SEASONAL PICTURE BOOKS *continued*

Fall

- ■ *Autumn* by Gerda Muller
- ■● *The Busy Little Squirrel* by Nancy Tafuri
- *Chipmunk Song* by Joanne Ryder, illustrated by Lynne Cherry
- *Christopher's Harvest Time* by Elsa Beskow
- *Flower Fairies of the Autumn* by Cicely Mary Barker
- ♥ *Goodbye Summer, Hello Autumn* by Kenard Pak
- ★ *Katya's Book of Mushrooms* by Katya Arnold with Sam Swope
- ★● *Leaf Man* by Lois Ehlert
- *The Mushroom Hunt* by Simon Frazer, illustrated by Penny Dale
- ♥ *My Autumn Book* by Wong Herbert Yee
- *Ox-Cart Man* by Donald Hall, illustrated by Barbara Cooney
- ♥ *Thanksgiving in the Woods* by Phyllis Alsdurf, illustrated by Jenny Løvlie
- *Woody, Hazel and Little Pip* by Elsa Beskow

Winter

- ★■ *Bear Snores On* by Karma Wilson,
- ● illustrated by Jane Chapman
- *Flower Fairies of the Winter* by Cicely Mary Barker
- ♥ *Goodbye Autumn, Hello Winter* by Kenard Pak
- ♥● *Grandmother Spider Brings the Sun* by Geri Keams, illustrated by James Bernardin
- ●★ *A Hat for Minerva Louise* by Janet Morgan Stoeke
- ♥ *Hiders Seekers Finders Keepers: How Animals Adapt in Winter* by Jessica Kulekjian, illustrated by Salini Perera
- ■ *The Mitten* by Jan Brett
- *Owl Moon* by Jane Yolen, illustrated by John Schoenherr
- ♥ *A Simple Christmas on the Farm* by Phyllis Alsdurf, illustrated by Lisa Hunt
- *Sleep Tight Farm: A Farm Prepares for Winter* by Eugenie Doyle, illustrated by Becca Stadtlander
- ♥ *Ten Ways to Hear Snow* by Cathy Camper, illustrated by Kenard Pak
- ♥ *Tracks in the Snow* by Wong Herbert Yee
- *Who Gets the Sun Out of Bed?* by Nancy White Carlstrom, illustrated by David McPhail
- *Whose Footprints Are These?* by Gerda Muller
- ■ *Winter* by Gerda Muller
- *Winter Lullaby* by Barbara Seuling, illustrated by Greg Newbold
- *Winter Sleep: A Hibernation Story* by Sean Taylor and Alex Morss, illustrated by Cinyee Chiu

KEY

- ■ Board books for youngest readers
- ★ Some of our family's all-time favorites
- ♥ Books that feature diverse characters or stories
- ● Books that don't include human depictions

Farming and the Natural World

♥ *Bring Me Some Apples and I'll Make You a Pie: A Story about Edna Lewis* by Robbin Gourley

★● *The Complete Brambly Hedge* by Jill Barklem

■● *Eating the Alphabet* by Lois Ehlert

★● *Farm Anatomy: The Curious Parts and Pieces of Country Life* by Julia Rothman

♥ *The Farm That Feeds Us: A Year in the Life of an Organic Farm* by Nancy Castaldo, illustrated by Ginnie Hsu

♥ *Harlem Grown: How One Big Idea Transformed a Neighborhood* by Tony Hillery, illustrated by Jessie Hartland

♥ *In the Garden* by Emma Giuliani

♥ *Gathering the Sun: An Alphabet in Spanish and English* by Alma Flor Ada, translated by Rosa Zubizarreta, illustrated by Simón Silva

★♥ *In a Nutshell* by Joseph Anthony, illustrated by Cris Arbo

Little Witch Hazel: A Year in the Forest by Phoebe Wahl

● *Sing a Song of Seasons: A Nature Poem for Each Day of the Year* edited by Fiona Waters, illustrated by Frann Preston-Gannon

♥ *Sonya's Chickens* by Phoebe Wahl

♥ *What's Cooking in Flowerville?: Recipes from Balconies, Rooftops, and Gardens* by Felicita Sala

★ *A Year around the Great Oak* by Gerda Muller

The Year at Maple Hill Farm by Alice and Martin Provensen

A Year in Our New Garden by Gerda Muller

For Slightly Older Kids

★♥ *The Birchbark House* by Louise Erdrich

● *By Ash, Oak and Thorn* by Melissa Harrison

The Children of Noisy Village by Astrid Lindgren, illustrated by Ilon Wikland

♥ *The Good Garden: How One Family Went from Hunger to Having Enough* by Katie Smith Milway, illustrated by Sylvie Daigneault

★ *James Herriot's Treasury for Children* by James Herriot

♥ *Osceola: Memories of a Sharecropper's Daughter* by Osceola Mays, collected and edited by Alan Govenar, illustrated by Shane W. Evans

♥ *Seedfolks* by Paul Fleischman, illustrated by Judy Pedersen

Shanleya's Quest: A Botany Adventure for Kids Ages 9 to 99 by Thomas J. Elpel, illustrated by Gloria Brown

Understood Betsy by Dorothy Canfield Fisher

● *The Wind in the Willows* by Kenneth Grahame

When my own kids were little, each week I chose a book or two that highlighted some element of the season we were experiencing on our farm, such as rain in April or falling leaves in October. I selected a mix of fanciful and more realistic narratives but aimed for books with accurate and realistic imagery of the natural world (even if there were also trolls or gnomes in the stories!). Many were about farming and gardening specifically, but I also selected books that dealt with other parts of the natural world or other ways to explore the outdoors. We read the books cuddled on the couch in the morning or before bed.

The BEST thing about family farming is...

Being able to regroup as a family for lunch at home together every single day.

HANAKO MYERS, MIDORI FARM

I wanted my children to see an echo of what they were experiencing in their own lives through these stories, but I also hoped to expose them to information about seasons and life beyond our own. Inevitably there'd be elements of these books that presented information about people, animals, and plants that differed in different places, and it was a wonderful way to broaden their horizons. For example, in winter we read quite a few books about snow even though snow falls only occasionally where we live in Oregon. And we learned that people in other parts of the world have different names for the same plants and mushrooms we are familiar with.

These books were among their first introductions to more scientific explanations of the world they explored every day. We learned about hibernation and how germination works. Reading these books together was a way to highlight our family's value of the natural world by helping us pay closer attention to the world around us and learn the names of the phenomena we observed. It was cozy and delightful to curl up with my children and share the love that originally drew my husband and me to farming.

After we read a book, I usually left it out on the coffee table for another week or two so my children could revisit it, looking at the pictures and, eventually, rereading it themselves. Though my children are now 10 and 13, I still pull out favorite books seasonally and put them in baskets in our living room so that the kids can revisit old favorites. They also make great (very easy) seasonal decorations when displayed on our nature table!

Obviously we read books about all kinds of topics over the years, but as a farm parent I always came back to our experience with the natural world and our work on the farm as a foundation of our life together.

DISCUSSION AND JOURNALING QUESTIONS

▶ *What is your favorite season of the year? Why?*

▶ *Do you have a favorite seasonal food or milestone associated with your favorite season? How might you add a simple layer of intentional celebration around that food or milestone with a special family meal or community gathering?*

▶ *What kinds of natural objects does your family like to collect? Can you dedicate a space in your home to display your collected treasures?*

▶ *Is there a time of year—a season, month, or holiday— that is consistently challenging for you or your family because of a heavy workload or extreme weather? How might you find a new way to interact with this season that helps it feels more positive? Are there any activities you can cut back on during this season to help offset the challenges?*

Arianna Thorn
Sky Island Farm
Humptulips, Washington

CHORES
AND
FARM
WORK

THE FIRST YEAR we hosted a potato-planting party on our farm, our children were four and one. We invited our customers and their families to help plant and then have a potluck. We weren't sure exactly how the whole process would go, but we set up everyone with a task that worked for them: Less mobile people cut potatoes, and mobile children and adults filled buckets and walked out to the prepared furrows to drop them in, one by one.

Our children jumped right in, carrying slightly smaller buckets and carefully placing their potatoes at a mostly even spacing down the rows. Though they were quite young, it was clear they already felt a sense of ownership and belonging to the farm and the work. They conferred with other children about the best strategy and kept going more or less as long as everyone else (with a few breaks to play). And in fall, when we began to dig those potatoes, they recognized the varieties we'd planted months before and were able to connect the work they'd done with the roasted potatoes we served at dinner. They knew that their hands could provide sustenance for their whole family.

From the moment they were born, our children were immersed in our farm and our work. While Casey and I found that we couldn't both work at full capacity with our children alongside (see Chapter 10 for some thoughts on childcare), we did provide as many opportunities as possible for them to join in the work—or, at the very least, to be present as much as was safe. Out of those experiences they steadily developed habits and skills, and eventually gained their own responsibilities on the farm.

HAVING REAL WORK IS IMPORTANT

For many children in America today, the opportunity to do real work is becoming increasingly rare. Julie Lythcott-Haims writes about this profound shift in her book *How to Raise an Adult: Break Free of the Overparenting Trap and Prepare Your Kid for Success*. Lythcott-Haims served as dean of freshman and undergraduate advising at Stanford University. As dean, she observed many students who seemed to lack important life coping skills, to the detriment of their college and eventual working experience, as well as their mental health and relationships. While undergraduate students at a highly selective college might seem like a rarified outlier population, Lythcott-Haims provides compelling evidence that young people across the board are starting adulthood unprepared to thrive—and she points to "overparenting" in its many forms as a primary cause.

Overparenting, in this context, is the phenomenon of parents attempting to keep their children safe and help them perform well in school—but ultimately protecting children from challenges and formative experiences that help build resilience, independent thinking, and a work ethic. Lythcott-Haims says changes in kids' play lives and lack of free time deprive them of opportunities to grow their imaginations and stretch their bodies. But she also stresses the importance of early responsibility and real work experiences in developing kids' confidence and an appreciation of their ability to contribute to the wider world.

These two experiences of play and work, while seemingly opposites, are closely linked in terms of their importance in children's growth. Both kid-directed play and real work teach kids essential lessons about agency and their own abilities. Whether it's hauling branches through a forest to build a fort or helping to harvest potatoes for dinner, a child engaging in constructive play or participating in physical work is learning that their actions make a positive difference. They can physically see (and even eat!) the results of their labors. They can also observe how others in their life benefit from their efforts when, for example, their friends play in the fort or their whole family enjoys eating the potatoes.

Making the connection between personal effort and outcome is a simple but profound realization, one that we may take for granted as adults but that needs to be learned through practice, practice, practice. It does not need to be a slog—good work can be fun and satisfying. To me, work and play live on the same continuum, often overlapping completely. If you are reading this book, it is likely that your work on your farm or homestead was driven at least at first by the creative impulse of play—the desire to be outside moving your body and starting interesting projects.

Many of the best forms of play require work and effort to yield the fullest rewards. Farming and gardening are just two examples, but musicians, athletes, chefs, and artists will also recognize that pursuing something they love has required them to have resilience, diligence, and commitment. One of my favorite definitions of confidence comes from *Design Matters* podcast host Debbie Millman. She has interviewed creatives from across industries about their work and process, and she says: "Confidence is the successful repetition of any endeavor."

Kids growing up on farms and homesteads live in an environment rich with opportunities to understand the connection between effort and resulting positive feelings—and that understanding is one of the best gifts we can give our children.

KIDS ARE READY WHEN THEY'RE READY

Watching my own kids and others, I have observed four basic stages to a child's participation in work, whether on the farm or around the home. I've labeled these stages Observing Work, Experimenting with Work, Helping with Real Work, and Working Independently. Though the stages outline a progression of involvement, children will continuously cycle through them for different kinds of work as they grow, learn new skills, and stretch themselves into new responsibilities.

Kids begin their immersion in work simply by being present and observing. Whether they are actively watching or not, a baby being carried in a sling while their parent collects eggs is getting a lesson in work. They can see the basic components: opening the hen house, eggs in nests, hands reaching in (sometimes under cranky broody hens!), eggs coming out, eggs going in a basket, the basket getting

THE LEGALITY OF KIDS AND FARM WORK

According to the US Department of Labor, "Minors of any age may be employed by their parents at any time in any occupation on a farm owned or operated by [their] parent(s)." Farm exemptions also exist in terms of what kind of work children can legally do at certain ages, and some states have exceptions for agricultural work in general.

That being said, child labor laws are in place to protect children, not only in terms of their bodily health and safety but also to provide them time to attend school, develop social lives, and pursue a wide variety of interests. So, while a family might not legally be bound to the laws when their own child is working, it's useful to know and understand the guidelines. (They are also useful to know when hiring young people to work on your farm.)

Here is a summary from the National Agricultural Law Center's website:

> Unless states pass their own rules, children who are 12 and older can work seven days a week outside of school hours with parental consent in any non-hazardous activity. Twelve is generally the minimum age for employment in agriculture. However, children under 12 can be employed in any non-hazardous agricultural job on a small farm outside of school hours with parental consent. Once children reach age 14, they may work any job on the farm that's defined as non-hazardous. Once they turn 16, they may legally work all farm jobs without restriction.

For the most recent guidelines and more details specific to your state, visit the Department of Labor's Youth & Young Worker Agricultural Employment website and the National Agricultural Law Center's website. (See Suggested Reading and Other Resources, page 222, for URLs.)

full. We take the basic logistics of such a simple task for granted, but it is a powerful lesson for a tiny human. They are learning the value of effort and the physical mechanics of work.

While working for extended periods with babies and small children is very challenging (see Chapters 9 and 10 for ideas on managing), on a farm there will still be many opportunities for even very young children to be present for some portion of work: harvesting from the garden for dinner, planting seeds in the greenhouse, picking apples, feeding the animals, and so on.

It was clear to Casey and me that our children were watching activity on the farm from a very young age. Even as toddlers they understood basic concepts such as how to walk in a path versus a planted bed and which parts of plants are edible. They learned by observing us. And we enjoyed talking to them about what we were doing, so that harvesting for dinner became a casual lesson.

Hanako Myers's son is only two, but he frequently accompanies Hanako or her husband, Marko Colby, when they do chores at Midori Farm in Washington. They also have on-farm childcare providers so that even when they are working, their son is present on the farm. As

Even young children learn about work from watching their parents.

a result of this simple proximity to their work, Hanako said, she feels like he already knows a great deal about the farm: "He's so interested in what everybody's doing and loves the farm. He knows what Marko and I each do every day. He might not be able to say it in paragraphs, but he knows what my role is, and he knows the places on the farm that I work, and he knows the places and things that Marko does and what sounds are associated with that."

EXPERIMENTING WITH WORK

The next stage is when kids start to want to help and pitch in without the obligation to finish a task. This is a big, long stage that begins quite early. When our oldest child was barely standing, he already wanted to mimic our actions, helping to dig sweet potatoes in the fields or cleaning dry onions in storage.

For the youngest children, this "help" is more akin to play. They are experimenting with the sensory experience of the soil when digging or feeling the papery-smooth wrappings on the onions. In the same way that seeing another child playing with a new toy will pique their interest, seeing their parent doing a new task will make them want to try it as well. But as they grow, they will want to engage in new work alongside you out of different levels of curiosity.

Obviously, safety concerns and work deadlines might make some tasks less conducive to a child's "help," but welcoming kids' efforts as much as possible will encourage them to continue being engaged with the work in a positive way. Adults need to navigate these opportunities with a mind toward the long-term goal of kids' learning balanced with short-term needs: Is this a moment when you can pause and explain and teach? Can you accept some sloppy work? Is this a safe activity for your child? Would it be better to invite them to help another time?

If children aren't naturally asking to pitch in, or if much of your work often isn't compatible with having a child present, you can invite them to participate when you are doing an activity you know will be well suited to them. In late winter, Casey always invited our children to help sow some of the first seeds of the season. Even though later sowings were more urgent, bigger scale, and less suited to kid hands, these first few flats were a kind of lighthearted celebration, and our children enjoyed helping from as young as two.

As they grow older, this kind of pitching in will become useful! Even young children can help pick peas. Depending on their age, they might help for a shorter or longer time, but it's important for kids to have opportunities to jump in and help only for as long as their interest holds. This will give them a wide variety of experiences and a sense of feeling free to try things without the commitment to finish a task. They can still run off and play and explore.

HELPING DO REAL WORK

At some point, kids become mature enough and skilled enough that it's appropriate to start asking them to help an adult or group fulfill an entire task. The extent to which they're ready for this level of work

KIDS AT WORK

Young children's efforts to "help" may be cute and sweet, sometimes frustrating, and usually *brief*. But repeated opportunities to be present for safe work can grow a future work ethic.

depends a lot on the task, the people they are with, and the context. For example, our children were able to keep on planting potatoes during our planting parties in part because there were other children also helping, the task wasn't too onerous, and they were given opportunities to take breaks.

The opportunity to be present for an entire task can help deepen a child's understanding of the work and provide a new opportunity for them to learn what it takes to do it well. Children's confidence in their own abilities can grow and flourish when they are given respectful feedback that assumes they can meet our expectations. For some reason, adults in recent years have hesitated in correcting children, but there is tremendous empowerment that comes from learning to

On a 1,400-acre farm, daily operations aren't necessarily kid-friendly. But Benina Montes's kids found many opportunities to help around Borroughs Family Farm, such as taking care of the family's sheep. "Kids are capable, so let them try and get their hands dirty and experience life," Benina said.

do a complex task correctly, and having our work adjusted through feedback is an essential part of that process.

Some of what we may need to teach our children might surprise us, because there are many skills to learn about life, farming, and being a responsible human in the world. For example, Christina Menchini's six-year-old son has occasionally helped her help load up and work at their Campfire Farms market booth. Even though he's quite young, he uses their point-of-sale system to help sell their pork products to customers. "The SKUs [stock-keeping units] have pictures, so he can enter the items," she said. "He knows where the weights are on each package, so he'll put in 1.12 pounds of bacon and ring people up." Because he's naturally shy and didn't initially want to talk to people while doing the work, Christina had to explain to him, "If you're going to sit on the stool and be customer facing and represent us, you have to talk to customers. You cannot just take their money and not say anything to them." Between his interest and her feedback, he is learning essential life skills about money, business, and how to interact professionally with strangers.

The scale and work of a farm will determine the scope of opportunities for a child to pitch in. Homesteads and smaller farms are often very well suited to this type of kid coworking arrangement, but even on larger farms there can be opportunities, especially around some of the "extra" projects farm families do around the house—keeping laying flocks, having their own home garden, or smaller side enterprises.

WORKING INDEPENDENTLY

As a result of helping around the farm their whole lives, Benina Montes's oldest children, 10 and 12 years old, team up to wash eggs on the weekends. The farm has about 3,000 laying hens and uses a mechanized flow-through egg washing system. "It's easier if there are two people, because that makes the whole system more efficient," she said. One loads, and the other unloads, checks quality, and packs. Benina pays them for their work. "They enjoy the spending money." Benina's oldest daughter also has her own small enterprise growing succulents. She has garden beds and pots with "mother plants" that she uses to propagate new plants for potted planters she designs and sells.

These are both examples of the ways children can eventually grow into having more independent responsibilities, taking on their own projects, and even working as paid employees on a farm crew. Again, some independent responsibilities can begin quite young; for example, many elementary-school-aged children will be ready to take on some daily animal chores and can usually complete these tasks on their own with some gentle reminding.

Bil Thorn and Kate Harwell's teenage children are very involved in the day-to-day operation of Sky Island Farm—at this point even helping plan the farming season and giving feedback on marketing strategies. Bil and Kate have expected their children to participate in farm work on some level ever since they were younger and living at a remote homestead. Though it sounds like they've expected a lot from their children, Bil said it's been important to ensure the experience is positive for their kids. "Make sure the tasks you ask the kids to perform aren't the worst tasks," he said. "Oftentimes we, the parents, take on the 'crap' tasks so that the kids can do things that are more enjoyable."

Corinne Hansch, whose teens contribute a lot of work to the family's Lovin' Mama Farm in New York, agrees. "I never make them do something that they really hate to do," she said, "but it's a balance because sometimes you just have to go to the chickens and close their house and feed them. We walk that line of pushing them to help and contribute while also respecting their needs, too. But, keeping them involved on the farm has always meant we get to spend more time with them even though we work so much." (Again, sharing work as a family builds a sense of belonging together.)

Once children are taking on independent responsibilities, it's important to keep checking in with them and providing supportive feedback. Be sure to demonstrate each task and then watch them do it. Make sure they truly understand what is expected of them, whether they're selling at market, bunching bouquets, or feeding animals. Support them as needed with tools, supplies, and lists or reminders. Say thank-you and acknowledge your appreciation of their contributions. These are all basic management techniques a farmer might use with an employee, and they are applicable with children, too. However, remember that even a farm-raised teenager is still growing and may not be ready for every task, especially anything that might carry physical risks.

Bil Thorn and Kate Harwell's teen daughter, Arianna Thorn, takes the lead on managing their farm's greenhouse and starts.

AGE-APPROPRIATE CHORES

Please use these suggestions for *ideas* of what tasks might be developmentally appropriate for children at different ages. Each individual child's maturity and capabilities will vary widely, even among children from the same family.

It's not safe (or fair!) to ask children to do work that they are not yet ready to do, so adjust your expectations to match specific children. On the flip side, some children may exceed your expectations when given the chance to take on more responsibility. Just keep in mind their size, strength, agility, and understanding of safety guidelines when you begin asking them to do

any work involving risk around machinery or animals. To reiterate what I've said elsewhere in this book, vehicles/equipment and large animals pose the biggest injury risks to children on farms.

Remember that children's attention spans and endurance for work will grow as they do. A three-year-old might enjoy helping harvest peas for dinner for about two minutes before wanting to quit and go play, whereas a 13-year-old who's getting paid might be able to pick multiple totes of peas for market. Also, it would be excessive to expect any child to do *all* of the work tasks I've suggested here, and some of the more advanced farming skills (such as operating a tractor or helping to manage other workers) might not ever interest your child(ren).

In these lists, I've included both farm- and home-based tasks, as they are equally important for children to learn to do as they grow.

Toddlers (1–3 years)

Children are interested in the world around them almost from birth, and once they can walk, toddlers will be curious about the tasks you do. These earliest years are about their safe exploration of the world. They can begin to help in an extremely limited way but will need constant supervision and a lot of forgiveness. Think of their "help" not as work but as a play/learning experience.

- Accompany adults or older children while they do nonhazardous work or chores
- Collect eggs (with help and supervision)
- "Help" harvest (with help and supervision)
- Feed pets (with help and supervision)

Preschool (3–5 years)

Motor and communication skills begin to develop rapidly in preschool-aged kids, but they are still quite young. They likely will want to help only for short periods and will need constant supervision and very friendly reminders of basic expectations (such as clearing their plate after dinner). Help them grow by giving them easy-to-accomplish tasks with a high success rate.

- Sow seeds into flats with supervision
- Help harvest for very brief sessions
- Put away their own toys and things at end of day (with help)
- Clear their own plate and utensils after meals (with reminders)
- Help dust, sweep, and clean the house

Elementary-school age (6–9 years)

In this age range, we see big changes in executive function and ability to follow through on tasks with less constant supervision or hands-on help, but this will vary *widely* from child to child. Continue to keep tasks brief for this age group and be prepared to provide regular gentle reminders. Once a child can read, you may find it helpful to post a daily schedule with a list of their expected tasks.

- Collect eggs and feed hens without supervision
- Complete daily chores for pets and/or small animals
- Help harvest for short sessions
- Help transplant starts
- Help weed the garden by hand or with a hoe
- Sow and water starts in a greenhouse
- Clear rocks from fields
- Help set up a market booth and keep it stocked
- Thin apples or other fruit (not on a ladder)
- Watch younger siblings with adults nearby
- Learn to safely use a knife to harvest
- Carry in firewood
- Prepare their own snacks and lunches
- Help cook dinner
- Load and unload the dishwasher
- Take out the garbage, recycling, and compost
- Help clean the house
- Bring in the mail
- Make their bed every morning
- Do their own laundry

Tweens (10–12 years)

In middle school, kids' bodies are getting bigger, and they are much more capable. Depending on the child, some kids may begin to have more interest in working longer periods on the farm, while others might go through a period of resisting work. They are also likely beginning puberty, which can be a time of inner development and turmoil, so be patient. They might seem almost like mini-adults one day and then act like toddlers the next. But continue to expect them to engage in reasonable regular work around the house and farm, because physical activity and responsibility can be very empowering during a time when their bodies might start to feel awkward or new to them.

- Harvest and do field work for longer periods—entire mornings or afternoons
- Complete daily chores for small and medium-size animals
- Prune and trellis berries
- Work point-of-sale at the market, adding up sales and making change
- Split kindling and build fires in a woodstove
- Help with brush removal at farm edges

Young teens (13–16 years)

Teenagers can be incredibly capable and knowledgeable, but they might also start to want more of a life off the farm. So be balanced in your expectations and remember that puberty continues, with all its potential for emotional turmoil. Even if they've grown up on the farm, continue to train teenagers carefully for new tasks, especially if you give them more significant responsibility and work with machinery.

- Work on the farm part-time, doing most tasks
- Watch younger siblings when adults are off the farm or working
- Begin learning how to safely use lighter-duty machinery and tools
- Work with large animals
- Prune orchard trees
- Move portable fencing
- Process firewood
- Prepare dinner for the household on a rotating schedule

Older teens (16+ years)

Older teens who want to continue working on the farm can be invaluable, often matching adults for physical skills and farming knowledge. But this is also the time when it might be important for them to explore life and careers beyond the farm (even if they might choose to come back later).

- Use tractors and heavy machinery (with proper training)
- Work full days on the farm when not in school
- Help coordinate and train other farm workers
- Take on management for specific parts of the farm (e.g., a greenhouse)
- Help develop the farm's website and manage social media marketing

Up until now I've extolled the benefit of farming and real work for children's development and growth, but I would be remiss if I didn't mention how valuable it can be to have more capable hands pitching in on a farm (and around the house)! Farming and homesteading are a ton of work, and often the little repeated tasks can add up to a lot of time—daily animal chores, watering starts in the greenhouse, weeding the garden. This is work that needs to be done, and not all of it is particularly hard. The same is true around the house: picking up toys, making lunch, clearing the table, doing laundry.

The sooner that children can begin helping with some of these little daily tasks on the farm and in the house, the easier *everyone's* life can become. There's more room for fun, new projects, and time together. Taking the time to teach children how to do these tasks can slow you down in the short run but pays off in the long run. Life is simply less stressful when there are more people to share the load.

Daisy Remington and her family learned this unexpectedly when she hurt her back in early 2020. Her son had just turned 12, and up until then he had a few small chores and helped on a more voluntary basis with caring for the many animals on their family's small New Zealand farm. But after her injury, she couldn't do most of the animal chores. With her husband away at his off-farm job during the day, her

The BEST THING about FAMILY FARMING is...

Seeing my kids now living on the farm we bought and their joy at running around outside, riding bikes, feeding the chickens. It makes it feel like all these growth years and all the associated pain and tears were worth it!

AMY FRYE, BOLDLY GROWN FARM

son picked up the work. "He was helping me raise two bottle calves, moving the cattle, and basically everything I do," she said. "I didn't know he was capable of doing everything I needed him to, but when the chips were down, he was like, 'Yep, I've got you.'"

DISCUSSION AND JOURNALING QUESTIONS

▶ *What chores or work did you do as a child and teenager? How did you respond to being asked to do your chores? How long did it take for you to become comfortable with the expectations? What skills do you remember learning?*

▶ *What chores or work do you currently expect of your child(ren)? How well matched do you think your expectations are with their current maturity? What is the balance between their work time, school time, and play time?*

▶ *What tasks do you think you could prepare your child(ren) for next? What skills do you want to make sure your children have before they leave home? What areas of the farm or home could use their help?*

LEARNING
AND
HOME-
SCHOOLING
ON THE FARM

LEARNING HAPPENS EVERY DAY for kids on a farm or homestead. They learn while they play and by watching the adults and older children in their lives work. They learn when they count change for customers at the market or read seed catalogs and help plan the garden. This kind of on-farm learning happens even for kids who go off-farm for school. For many farm families, sending their children to school is absolutely the right choice for their children's academic careers (and for parents who might not want to carry the responsibility of being parents, farmers, *and* teachers).

But some homesteading and farming families choose to focus all of their children's education on home- and farm-based learning. Homeschooling is legal in most places today, and resources to support it have proliferated in the past decade, making this option more accessible than ever for families. What can the choice to homeschool look like on a farm?

A SAMPLE HOMESCHOOLING DAY

Here's a snapshot of a typical day of homeschooling (and also farming!) when my children were younger: On a quiet late-September morning, I wake when Rusty and Dottie tumble into bed with me in the early hours. We snuggle for a few minutes and chat about our day to come, and then we all wander downstairs, where Casey has just come in from moving irrigation pipe. He makes breakfast with eggs from our hens and greens he harvested on his way back from the fields, while I check the farm email to see if any customers have questions about our CSA delivery that day. We harvested most of the vegetables on our CSA list yesterday, and they are washed and packed in the cooler, but Casey heads out after breakfast to pick a few last items, and the kids and I jump into our morning school routine around eight thirty a.m.

We start our homeschool days on the couch reading. I read aloud to them from books about history or mythology, from novels, from books of poetry, and more. After I read, I ask them to take turns telling back what they heard. Then I take turns with each of them at the kitchen table, working on their phonics or spelling or math. When they need a "brain break," they go run around outside to explore, harvest apples for a snack, say hi to Papa, and dig in their giant pit. We finish most of our daily school goals by lunch.

Casey has been working on the farm all morning, finishing the harvest, sowing winter greens, and weeding. After lunch, the children go to my parents' house for the afternoon and evening, and I join Casey in the truck as we haul our week's harvest to the downtown storefront where we meet our CSA customers. We arrive back home at the kids' bedtime, put them to bed, and then eat a late dinner before falling into bed ourselves.

This has been a full day, with farm work and life occurring side by side with lessons that happen both organically and by design.

CHOOSING TO HOMESCHOOL

Homeschooling styles and approaches are unique for every family. Ours has evolved over time. As of the writing of this book, our family has homeschooled for eight years, starting when my oldest was kindergarten age. We reconsider our choice every school year, and for us it has been the right choice so far.

We were first inspired to try homeschooling by the homeschooling families we'd met through our farming experiences. The farmer we trained with in Bellingham, Washington, had three children who learned at home for parts of their childhood (one of them is featured in Chapter 14).

Another practical reason some farmers choose homeschooling is because of how busy summers can be on the farm. Many non-farming families might choose to spend extra time together in summer because that's when school is on break. Instead, homeschooling farm families often look forward to time spent together in the quieter off-season as they read books or do math lessons by the fire.

5 DAILY LEARNING
EXPERIENCES

1 Let them work with you.

Depending on the age of your child, this may require extra patience and letting go of some expectations of how much you can get done, but it can be a huge educational experience. Corinne Hansch said that one of their favorite homeschooling experiences was building a small greenhouse together as a family. "My husband, Matthew, got out the measuring tape and paper on a clipboard and taught them the Pythagorean theorem to get the corners right."

2 Walk in your fields.

Don't have an agenda for this one—no plans to harvest or to teach anything. Just simply invite your child(ren) on a walk and see what you find. Even with older children, I am amazed at the things we see, and also the conversations we can have, while aimlessly strolling around our property.

3 Watch for wildlife and seasonal changes.

Our earliest "science" lessons on our farm were all based on the natural world right outside our door. We keep out several regional field guides of birds, wildlife, and plants (including weeds!) and watch for what we can spot on our farm and how these change over time. We keep bird feeders by our house and have learned what seasons different birds visit.

4 Read related books.

Reading books *about* farming or the seasonal changes in the natural world can be a valuable way to increase your child's awareness of the experiences they're having throughout the day and how they fit into the wider context of learning and the world. Reading aloud is also an important part of early literacy, and even older children can benefit from being read to. They often understand more advanced writing and topics when they are read aloud and can discuss content or learn the meaning of new words. Plus, it's an easy and delightful way to bond and share time with your children. (See Chapter 3 for a list of suggested books.) For more about the educational power of reading aloud and a treasury of other great books, I highly recommend *Jim Trelease's Read-Aloud Handbook* by Jim Trelease and Cyndi Giorgis.

5 Play a game!

Finally, as farmers, let's be honest—sometimes we want to create a more intentional learning opportunity with our kids but are too tired from a day of work (or farming emergencies) to facilitate something creative. Board and card games are perfect ways to help kids learn new concepts and skills such as basic math. For younger children (and siblings!), I recommend choosing non-competitive or cooperative options to avoid meltdowns around losing.

Corinne Hansch was inspired to pursue a home-based and integrated life when she did a hospice training course in high school. "I worked with people who were dying at home, and that experience opened my mind to that fact that transformative life events can happen at home."

USING THE FARM AS A RESOURCE

Farmers who work at home have a rich educational environment for fostering learning. Again, learning can happen organically throughout a day of doing chores and farm work. When deciding whether to homeschool, Casey and I saw that right outside awaited millions of learning and play opportunities for our children. Corinne Hansch and her husband, Matthew, homeschool their three children on Lovin' Mama Farm in New York, and Corinne agreed: "The farm is definitely the classroom, and a lot of learning happens on the farm. We have faith that the environment they're growing up in is very valuable and truly unique."

When Diane Saleh and her husband started their farm, Halal Pastures, in New York, they knew it would be a core part of their children's learning experience. Their children have been able to pursue topics that fascinate them right on the farm. Their daughter was interested in mushrooms one year. "We identified every mushroom that grows on the farm," Diane said. "She learned about fungi and their contributions to the soil out of her own interest." Meanwhile, Diane's young sons are fascinated by the farm's tractors. "I went to the library and picked out a book on tractors for elementary-school kids," she said. "We got the tractor out and learned, 'This is the hydraulics arm, the bucket, the cab . . . here it is in the book.'"

MAKING TIME AND SPACE FOR LEARNING

If you decide that homeschooling is the right choice for your family, you will need to be intentional about making the time and space for learning in your lives. Keep in mind that learning at home can look very different than it does in a school because much of school routines are built around maintaining order and educating many same-age students at once!

At home, the process is very different. When given one-on-one attention or materials designed for independent use, children can often learn key academic skills such as math, reading, and writing in shorter periods of instruction time each day. Students can also (eventually) take more responsibility for their own subject-based learning, often through reading books about topics such as history or science rather than listening to classroom lectures or presentations. While there are many ways to help children learn at home, two key ingredients are necessary with any approach: making time and space.

"We made a conscious decision that the farming was going to be their homeschooling. Homeschooling cannot be separate from the farm—it's one and the same for us."

—DIANE SALEH

Home learning doesn't require the same regimented schedule or tailored classroom space we might recognize from school. But it is important to build rhythms to make sure learning happens. Although her kids are more independent now, Corinne Hansch said that in the early days, she and Matthew would "tag team" homeschool, usually getting the work done by the end of the morning. When their kids tackled lessons on more challenging subjects, like math, "they needed our attention 100 percent," she said. That meant only one parent was available for farm work unless they recruited another friend or family member to help with school (which they did occasionally!).

Our family has taken a similar approach, with mornings during the school year reserved for our lessons four days a week, but that time is usually bookended by farm work. There are other ways to organize the routines, of course. Perhaps your family works on learning year-round, and so you spend less time facilitating lessons every week. If that works and students are making progress, the time element is flexible. But still, homeschooling will take time.

So loosen your farming or homesteading schedule to accommodate that process, and consider your seasonal schedule. What's your slowest season, and how can you make it a special "learning season," when you and your children dig in deeper with books? Likewise, during your busier seasons, how can you be more conscious of helping the children learn from the work you are doing on the farm?

Even with seasons designated for school, many homeschooling farm families find that lessons get interrupted. "Nature's out there, and it does what it wants to do," Daisy Remington said about teaching her two children at her New Zealand farm. "I'll think we're going to have a great school day, and then I'll see that our calf is sick. And suddenly everything is out the window and has to change. So, our schooling has to be very fluid." Prioritizing *some* key lessons every day can be a better way to make consistent progress than setting unrealistic goals.

Homeschooling can take place in any setting.

Home learning also takes space, mostly because it takes supplies! Our family has never had a dedicated school room in our small house—we always "do school" on our couch and at the dining table—but I do have a few small shelves and baskets in our living room dedicated to storing whatever books we're reading, pencils and art materials, board games, and other supplies. Having dedicated space is another way for our family to remember that learning is one of our goals. And because the space is limited, I always aim to keep it current with what each child needs at that time.

FOLLOWING YOUR KIDS' LEAD

Homeschooling on a farm or homestead is especially well suited to very practical, hands-on subjects such as math and science, many of which are parts of everyday farm work and life. Diane Saleh said that in her chidren's early years, the farm provided more than enough of this kind of practice. "A lot of the basic concepts like counting happen in farming," she said. "'How many seeds do I need to put in this

> *"I decided farming and tending of the land would be the majority of our school. We asked questions like: How much sunlight does this plant need? How much sunlight do we have now? Where's the sunlight coming from?"*
>
> —DAISY REMINGTON

tray?' And they learn the anatomy of the body. When we butcher an animal, they can see what the insides look like in the cavity."

Daisy said that the practical nature of learning on the farm is very effective for her children. "Because both of my kids are on the autism spectrum, many times they really truly must have a concrete, tangible example of the thing," she said. Her son understands things best when they are something he can see. For him, learning is, as Daisy said, "show me the concrete example of how this is true or else it is not true."

As a result, Daisy emphasizes the farm in their homeschooling, supplementing with materials to cover the basics of reading, writing, and math. "Eighty percent of their school is actually just being on the farm," she said. "Everything is applicable or can give them an example, whether it's a story of something we did on the farm or actually something in front of us."

Learning at home can provide flexibility for tailoring the experience to meet many kinds of special needs, so long as parents feel equipped to support their child. Many homeschoolers team up with support through local public schools or online or community resources to help design appropriate learning plans.

Homeschooling can also provide time and space for children to actively pursue more interests, whether those are spending more time with some aspect of farming or having time to take classes off the farm. My children have both fallen in love with music, and now that they are 10 and 13, we take them to private music lessons or orchestra rehearsals twice a week. They also practice their instruments for up to an hour a day. It's a big commitment, and it would be harder for them to dedicate that amount of time in addition to a full day spent at school. As it is, they have time in their days to do their schoolwork, play and practice music, and help with chores around the house and farm while still having plenty of time for free play and reading.

Homeschooled kids can spend as much time as they want pursuing their passions.

CREATING A HOMESCHOOL COMMUNITY

Once they get past the "how to" part, a common concern for home-schooling parents is finding a community so that children can have friends and develop social skills. Homeschooling families typically do this by building rich social opportunities into their lives, and, of course, farm kids often have extra people in their lives beyond their families—for example, employees and customers.

Corinne Hansch takes her kids with her to the market. "Fifteen thousand people come through every weekend," she said, "so they're getting exposed to interacting with total strangers. They're very confident talking with any age group, from babies to elders." Her teens also work side by side with their farm's hired employees and have formed positive relationships with them. "The kids really love having other adults around," she said.

In terms of finding peers and friends, many communities have active homeschooling groups or co-ops that meet regularly. For years, our children attended a nearby weekly "farm school" program, which provided an opportunity for them to meet other kids and experience being more independent from their parents (and it gave me at least one day a week when I could focus all my attention on other work!).

Farm kids, whether homeschooling or not, can join local farm clubs like 4-H or Future Farmers of America (FFA) to connect with other kids interested in farming or crafts. These programs are excellent ways to structure a farm kid's first independent projects, such as raising their own farm animals. Showing animals or entering produce in the local county fair can provide an opportunity to share their work with the wider community and get positive feedback.

Farmers and homesteaders can also build those connections by hosting such groups and classes on their own farms. We participated for many years in a parent-run homeschooling co-op and often hosted social and educational events on our farm for the group. For several years, we hosted a lantern walk in fall that gave town kids their first opportunity to walk outside in a truly dark environment. We also had a wildlife biologist teach the co-op kids about birds on our land.

Diane Saleh offers a more formal 10-week summer program at Halal Pastures. Kids and their families come one day per week to learn about farm chores and life, how to grow food, the science of farming, and more. Hosting the students and their families provides Diane's own children more social and learning opportunities, too.

"When the kids come here on their first day, they're afraid of the bugs," Diane said. "Some of them don't know that eggs come from chickens—basic things like that." They end the final week with a meal from the farm, and at that point the students and their families will have participated in growing the vegetables. "The kids walk away with a greater understanding of food and the environment and what it takes to make it."

DISCUSSION AND JOURNALING QUESTIONS

▶ *What are your children's current educational options? How do you feel about them? What are the pros and cons?*

▶ *Would you like your children to be educated more formally, or are you interested in teaching them at home?*

▶ *Take an honest assessment of your life and work: Do you have time and space to homeschool?*

▶ *What are some ways in which you see your children already learning on the farm? What are their current interests? How can you support them in pursuing those interests?*

Christina Menchini
Campfire Farm
Mulino, Oregon

FINDING
BALANCE
AND ADDRESSING
STRESS

ONE GOAL OF this book is to help readers find a healthy balance between two enormous life roles—farming and parenting—but it's important to talk about this concept more specifically and in detail.

In my experience, it's often easier to identify when life is out of balance than to notice when it's not. By "out of balance," I mean having too many competing demands and costs, leaving us stretched way past what's comfortable in terms of our time, money, and energy budgets. We may feel chronically exhausted and worried, which we commonly call "being stressed." I like thinking of such things as a matter of balance, because we're never going to eliminate all stressors. They are a natural part of life, and certainly part of both parenting and farming. But, with intention, we can work toward a life that is more *balanced*, where we find space to rest and connect so that we are nourished and prepared to properly handle the inevitable hard stuff.

After my husband had major surgery soon following our daughter's birth, he just kept working—it was a hard time.

OUR OUT-OF-BALANCE STORY

When I reflect on our lives, it is easy to identify those painful moments when Casey and I were doing way too much. We've had many challenging periods on our farm, but sometimes we managed to weather those challenges and at other times it felt like we were barely making it through our days.

Our second child was born in September, the main season for harvesting, weeding, and planting for the upcoming fall and winter on our year-round farm. We had just added more acreage to our management and were gearing up to start our "full diet" style of CSA the first week of the next calendar year. We were adding new enterprises, taking care of animals, and scaling up all around. When it came time to pay bills and do payroll for our employees every week, my heart raced with anxiety; I was never quite sure we'd have enough money to cover all our expenses.

My daughter's birth was a hard one, requiring emergency care and leaving me severely anemic and physically exhausted. It took months for me to feel physically "normal" again. My bonding with my baby was delayed, and nursing hormones and chronic sleep deprivation took a big toll on my emotional state.

Meanwhile, Casey was needed on the farm every waking minute. He would head out at five in the morning to milk our cows, leaving me in the house with our newborn and our two-year-old son. Our older child was an early waker and inevitably woke the baby and me, too. So I'd find myself sitting downstairs with an awake baby and toddler at six, having hardly slept the night before. The toddler was occasionally aggressive toward the new baby, meaning I couldn't put her down anywhere and needed to keep an eye on both of them constantly during the day. I didn't even feel like I could make myself breakfast without help. I would sit in our (*very* messy) living room in those dark early-morning hours, hold my baby (who was always nursing), and quietly cry.

Then, a month after our daughter's birth, Casey was diagnosed with an aggressive melanoma that required major surgery. After the surgery, he barely rested; we just kept pushing as much as we could every day to get the work done, keep our kids fed, and try to survive.

BALANCE IS A GOAL

We did survive, of course! And as our children grew and we caught up with our scale, we eventually found more breathing room. When I look at family photos from that time, I can see the weariness and fatigue on our faces, but I also see the joy we felt in being immersed in our growing family and farm. Though our life at that time was beyond exhausting, it's hard to say we made the wrong choices.

Even then, though, we knew we needed to steer our family and farm toward something more sustainable. We

Our joy in our children has helped us weather many difficulties.

needed a life that provided us time to sleep and rest and connect, and enough money to pay the bills. We knew that balance was our goal.

And, perhaps, balance is always a *goal*. Because a life with growth and inevitable unexpected challenges (such as health crises) *will* cause us stress and shift how we spend our time and money. But, with awareness, we can intentionally steer our farm families back toward a life that is both challenging and restorative.

KIDS FORCE YOU TO FIND BALANCE

Having children can be a strong incentive to find work/life balance. Though having a family adds more moving parts and work to farm life, many farmers told me it also forced them to find balance in new ways.

Before we had kids, Casey and I worked long days without question. We'd start working immediately after breakfast, keep going until dark, finally coming inside and eating a simple dinner before bed. We were together and we enjoyed our work, so at the time it didn't *feel* like a problem to work all day. But it certainly wasn't sustainable for both of us to work at that pace with kids, and we were startled to find ourselves savoring the slowdown that came after our son's birth. Even during my pregnancy, we went on more walks again and enjoyed talking about things other than farming.

Hanako Myers and Marko Colby had a similar experience. They had been operating Midori Farm in Washington for more than a decade before adopting their son in 2020. "Out of necessity, we created an operation that worked when Marko and I each worked full days, six days a week, and then a few hours on Sundays," Hanako said. She said they still both put in long hours, but becoming parents has forced them to make changes in how they get everything done—and it also radically changed their perspective. "Having a child has forced us to 'punch out' of work, which is always difficult when operating your own business," Hanako said.

"Even if other people are still working on the farm, I am going for a bike ride with my child or taking him to the river, and I don't feel guilty about it. In that way, I feel like I have more balance in my life than I ever have, because I was never able to 'punch out' before I became a parent."

—HANAKO MYERS

She and Marko now both work clearly delineated hours, equally sharing parenting time and farming work as well as having childcare on the farm throughout the week. When they are done for the day, they focus on family.

LEARN TO LET GO

Again, we're not going to be able to avoid all stressors or challenges in our lives—that's not reasonable or even desirable, since stress often accompanies growth and new projects. But during those times of life when we feel excessively strained or overburdened, it can help ease the load to pause and see if there's anything we can let go of—even temporarily—to give ourselves more room or time.

I encourage people who are expecting babies to make that kind of room in their lives *before* the babies arrive—for example, cutting back on the number of markets. But often stressors arrive without

When Bil Thorn and Kate Harwell of Sky Island Farm in Washington found themselves working at an unsustainable pace—all day, every day—in the summer season, they decided to cut out farmers' market sales and focus more effort on wholesale orders, which allows them to take one day off every week.

warning or we take on more than we can handle without realizing how big the load will feel. At that point, perhaps it's possible to quickly look around the farm and see if there's an enterprise or project that can be paused.

Perhaps Casey and I should have paused our expansion efforts when he was diagnosed with cancer. But there are sometimes other ways to let go without interrupting physical projects. Namely, we can let go of (or at least reprioritize) our expectations—of our family, our farm, and our home life. Are our children fed and have they been hugged today? Are the animals fed and cared for? Have we harvested and delivered to our customers? Have we paid our employees on time? These are all important goals.

Less important goals in hard times might be having a photo-ready farm, family, or house. While that might seem like a small thing to let go of, so many of us document our lives for public consumption in ways that affect how we spend our time and how we judge our own lives. It's okay to have a messy house and weedy fields. Most of us do, at least some of the time.

It's also okay to prioritize your own individual needs, in this or other areas. Amy Frye at Boldly Grown Farm, for example, budgets for a house cleaner to help keep her family's home in order. "It is a luxury, but it's something we prioritize because we know how critical it is to our well-being," Amy said. "And the only reason we tidy up anything is because we know she's coming."

PRIORITIZE YOUR GOALS

On a farm, there is so much we *could* do—but it's important to accept that we can't do everything. Carla Emery's book *The Encyclopedia of Country Living* was an important inspiration to Casey and me in our early days of farming. It's full of information about homesteading and gardening arts: how to can tomatoes, milk goats, make cheese, dry herbs, prune berry canes, and much more. But Emery made a point to tell her readers that while she's done most of these things at some point in her life, she never did all of them in one year. In fact, she estimates that if a person were to do everything in her book in the same season, it would take 200 hours a day (or more!) to accomplish all the tasks. As a reminder: We only get 24 hours, and 8 of them should be spent sleeping.

Picking our priorities has certainly been the reality for us on our farm and homestead. Most years we've grown most of the basic vegetable crops, but something always gets dropped because of a seed failure or a farmer mistake or weather vagary. Likewise, some years we manage to freeze raspberries, some years we freeze blueberries, and some years we freeze both—or neither. I stopped canning completely soon after our second child was born, because working in a hot, steamy summer kitchen with boiling pots and kids running around stretched me way too thin. Now we freeze tomatoes and other crops for winter instead.

5 WAYS TO CONNECT
AND REFRESH

1 Get off the farm together.

The farm and/or homestead is the foundation of work life, home life, and so much joy. But in a busy farming life, it can be easy to spend all your time on the farm. "We try to make the farm our life. We try to make where we live also a place where we play," Diane Saleh of Halal Pastures in New York said. "But sometimes you just need to take some time off and take a breather. You're able to see things differently and take a step back."

Leaving the farm can be as simple as taking a hike or attending kids' sports games, but scheduling off-site extended vacations can be worth the work of making the space and finding a farm sitter. Lyn Jacobs and her husband, Juvencio Argueta, run La Finquita del Buho in Oregon, and they aimed to take their three children to visit Juvencio's family in Honduras once a year. Leaving their farm in someone else's hands brought mixed results. "We always had some sort of heinous disaster while away," Lyn said. "But the travel was very important to us, so we prioritized it."

2 Schedule some time off.

Hanako Myers and her husband, Marko, live a tightly scheduled work and family life at Midori Farm in Washington, which makes it possible for them to run their farm operation and be parents. "I can look at the calendar months down the road and tell you exactly what I'll be doing from five to six p.m., and what Marko will be doing, and who's going to pick up our son from our childcare at noon on Tuesday, April 4, and so on." This level of scheduling eliminates a lot of daily discussions about work and ensures that they each have nonwork time to spend with their son and as a family.

3 Establish occasions for connection.

In addition to making sure they have some time off, many farmers also intentionally schedule simple opportunities for connecting with their children and/or partner. For many farm families, together time is already built into farm life, but working together or seeing each other at meals doesn't always provide all the connection a family or partner needs or wants. With intention, simple family times can be built into your life: weekly game nights on dark winter evenings, for example, or a regular date night (perhaps even just a picnic near the house if the kids are old enough to be left alone with a radio or baby monitor), family bike rides or hikes, or a movie and pizza on a weekend evening.

4 Reach out beyond the farm.

Several years ago, I realized that most of my relationships were centered around the farm: My friends were our customers, our employees, and my family. So, I connected with an old friend who lives about as far away from our Oregon farm as possible: in Brooklyn, New York! She and I started a weekly phone date that provides an easy way to stay

in touch amid our busy family and work lives. I can put in earbuds and chat with her while making dinner, weeding the garden, or folding laundry. Having someone in my life who cares about me but isn't directly involved in the farm provides an important emotional outlet.

5 Budget for joy opportunities.

Part of what draws farmers to our work is a natural curiosity and desire to build new things. If farming is starting to feel stale, perhaps it's time to experiment with a new crop—maybe one that doesn't seem profitable (yet) but has the potential to bring big joy. On our farm, we have a concept we call "Casey's acre," where my husband can tinker each season by trying out different crops or growing methods. Sometimes these experiments become staple and profitable parts of our ongoing operation, and sometimes they are just for fun, but continually experimenting has helped Casey keep his joy for farming over many years.

What feels like "too much" will vary from person to person, of course, but we can let some things go in all years—especially in the hard ones.

Katrina McQuail is the primary farmer at Meeting Place Organic Farm in Ontario and a parent to three young children. In this season of her life, she has accepted that she's not going to meet all her professional goals in the next few years. "There are things that need to change for this year," she said. "And there are things that I know I want to do long-term, and we can inch toward those goals, but I don't need to make them happen right now."

STRESS CAN BE DANGEROUS

While it's normal to feel out of balance sometimes, it's also important to watch for signs of long-term or acute stress that causes actual harm. Rural sociologists Shoshanah Inwood and Florence Becot reached out to dozens of farm families to ask them about points of stress in balancing farming, family, and childcare. Many of the participants reported stress, but Shoshanah and Florence spoke with a few who reported extreme burnout and signs of untreated mental illness.

WATCH FOR THE DANGER SIGNS

Chronic or acute stress, if left unresolved, can lead to burnout or exacerbate disorders such as depression and anxiety. The only way to work toward balance is to recognize when we (or others) aren't doing well and begin to act.

Signs of stress, anxiety, and depression

- Persistent negative emotions
- Feeling hopeless about the future
- Loss of interest in previously enjoyable activities or work
- Insomnia and poor-quality sleep
- Physical symptoms such as back-aches, headaches, nausea
- Reduced attention to work, deadlines, commitments
- Reduced care for self or others (including animals)
- Increased accidents
- Change in eating habits
- Agitation and confusion
- Shifts in communication style (shorter temper)

- Withdrawal from existing relationships
- Increased drug/alcohol use
- Thoughts or talk of physically harming oneself or others

RESOURCES IN THE UNITED STATES FOR HELP IN A CRISIS:

- Farm Aid: Call the hotline at 1-800-FARM-AID (1-800-327-6243) or visit farmaid.org to fill out a help request email

- National Suicide and Crisis Lifeline (available 24 hours/day): Call/text 9-8-8 or visit 988lifeline.org to find more resources and chat online

- In an emergency, call 9-1-1

For more information, check out the Western Region Agricultural Stress Assistance Program. (See Recommended Reading and Other Resources, page 222.)

Sources: *How to Talk with Farmers under Stress*, by Paola Bacigalupo Sanguesa and David Thompson. Michigan State University Extension, June 19, 2019. *How Stress Affects You*, by Jinnifer Ortquist. Michigan State University Extension, June 19, 2019.

The BEST thing about family farming is...

Reaching our goals as a family, experiencing fresh food we grew ourselves, hearing my kids say they love growing food.

SARAH KOSTYU, K7 FARM

Shoshanah described to me an experience she had in a focus group of farm families: "The dad said, 'We've got three kids, we're homeschooling, and we have a diversified farm, and it's great.' Then he left the room, and the mother told me, 'I can't do this anymore.' She was really worried about harming herself or her kids." Overall, the researchers' surveys have confirmed that the combination of farming and parenting can be very stressful—in a 2023 survey they did of 860 farm and ranch families, 88 percent reported that stress and anxiety increased since children arrived.

Rachel Van Boven has also talked with many farmers experiencing crises through her work at Farm Aid's Farmer Hotline. Rachel grew up in a family of farmers and has worked on farms herself. She combines that experience with training and resources as she answers calls and emails from farmers with all kinds of needs—including farmers experiencing extreme stress. She says the hotline gets "everything from 'I want to quit my office job and be a farmer—how do I start?' to 'I'm about to lose my fifth-generation farm. Can you help?'" Her job is to listen and, when appropriate, connect farmers to resources that can offer the specific kind of help they need.

She said that financial stress and relationship stress are big reasons people call. "This last year we got a lot of calls related to both the drought and the rising costs of inputs," she told me when we spoke in early 2023. "So that's the initial reason they call, and then you dig in or just listen to the sound of their voice or listen to the underlying tone of their email." If farmers sound like they're really struggling, she'll ask them outright whether they're suicidal and connect them with immediate resources for support.

Katrina McQuail and her husband are fortunate to have both sets of parents living nearby and helping to support their family.

CREATE A NETWORK OF SUPPORT

In addition to reaching out to professionals for support, Rachel also recommends building community to find ongoing support and balance from friends and other farmers who might be able to relate to your experiences. "When we talk about farm stress and mental health, we don't talk enough about how isolation contributes to creating farm stress. And community is important in combating farm stress," she said. "There can be so much power in just having someone listen compassionately. Sometimes more is needed, but there's so much that can be met in community."

Researchers Florence and Shoshanah observed that the farmers in their focus groups expressed gratitude for hearing personal stories from other farmers about the realities of family life. Sometimes just knowing that your struggles are shared by others can be an important step in easing any stress around feelings of failure to get everything done.

As part of one focus group of 108 women, they asked the participants to share personal photos and stories. "We gave them prompts for sharing. Show us what your house looks like. Share what your stressors are," said Shoshanah. She said participants from very different types of farming were surprised at the similarities in their challenges. "At the end, women said, 'I don't feel alone.'" These kinds of experiences can happen within communities of farmers and parents locally, too.

When Katrina McQuail first moved back to help run Meeting Place Organic Farm, where she had grown up, she knew she wanted to build a local community of other women doing similar work. What started as a group of women farmers evolved into a group of women entrepreneurs who still meet years later. "Everyone's in different places and working on different things, but it's been a real opportunity to just share about the challenges of parenthood as well as the awesomeness of it," she said. "And then still have an identity outside of it."

Support from friends and family can be especially important during the hardest seasons of life. John McCafferty's wife died unexpectedly when their daughter was only eight months old. They were already homesteading on their 30 acres in New Zealand but weren't growing much commercially, and he spent several years envisioning what would come next for the land in his new reality as a single father. "In that space, I learned to lean on other people a lot," John said. "And I think that's really benefited me to this day. I wasn't good at asking for help before she died, and afterward I had to be."

With hands-on and emotional support to help get him through those very tough first few years, John was able to take care of his daughter and slowly build up Pleasant River Produce, a commercially viable farming enterprise. His farming operation allowed him to be with his daughter, take care of the land, and provide an income. Eventually he even met a new partner with whom he now has two more children. Life looks very different for him today, but John said that seeking and accepting support was essential in getting through that earlier hard time, and they still have help from their extended family and friends. "If you can find support, it makes farming while parenting a lot easier," John said. "I think for me it would be impossible otherwise."

DISCUSSION AND JOURNALING QUESTIONS

▷ *What are your current ideas about what it means to be a "farm family"? Are those ideas helpful or harmful to you?*

▷ *Close your eyes and think about your family's life as it is right now. How do you feel in your body? Can you identify any feelings of anxiety about certain elements? Are there missing pieces of connection that you need to find room to foster? Are you doing okay?*

▷ *If your life feels out of balance, where might you cut back on your expectations and work, either permanently or temporarily?*

▷ *What is one new simple connection or rest activity that you could sustainably add to your family's weekly or monthly rhythm?*

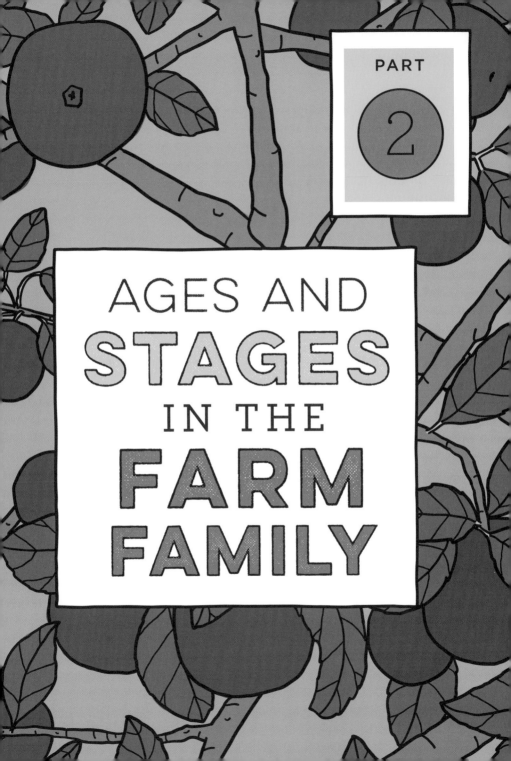

PART

2

AGES AND
STAGES
IN THE
FARM
FAMILY

Jacob Slosberg and Amy Frye
Boldly Grown Farm
Bow, Washington

PREPARING FOR THE
PARENTHOOD
JOURNEY

CHOOSING IF AND WHEN TO START A FAMILY is one of the most personal and important decisions a person or couple will make. Though it is rarely a simple decision for anyone, for people operating a farm, there are some unique factors to consider.

Casey and I always knew we wanted to raise a family, but when we started our farm in our mid-20s, that reality felt very far away. We had many pressing goals with our business and farm. For three whole years, our days were full from the moment we woke until we fell asleep. There was barely time for us to take care of *ourselves*, let alone another tiny human. But toward the end of our third season, we started to have breathing room. And in that breathing room, we realized that we'd grown up quite a lot since starting the farm. We no longer felt as much like "kids," and we could imagine ourselves taking on the responsibility of parenthood.

That December, we were snowed in on the farm. It was beautiful, but we were without internet or power, had to miss holiday plans with family, and felt isolated, lonely, and slightly bored. We looked out at

> *"We decided to blow up our lives and make a big career change from being chefs to farmers because we wanted to have a family. We knew there was no way both of us could work late nights in a kitchen—that lifestyle wasn't conducive to being parents."*
>
> **—JORDAN GOLDSMITH**

the white wonderland and said, "This snow would be a lot more fun with a kid." And so we began the process that led to us welcoming our son to the world one year later.

ARE YOU READY? (AND DOES IT MATTER?)

While Casey and I were able to establish many elements of our farm business before having our first child, there are many ways to approach this big decision. We could have justified waiting longer to better establish our farm—and, honestly, the farm would probably have benefited from more completely focused years of our energy. But the reality is, there's never a perfect time. This is the message I've heard from countless farmers who have become parents. Even if you wait until the farm is established and you have money in the bank, the transition to parenthood will still be a profound change with unforeseeable challenges and consequences.

Katrina McQuail of Meeting Place Organic Farm in Ontario said that she and her husband, Ben, started trying to have a baby when she was 35. "We were ready in our relationship and in our life stage and age to have kids," she said. At that point, she'd already spent four years operating the livestock farm founded by her parents decades earlier. "I'm really fortunate that I took over a farm business that was already incredibly well established," she acknowledged. But even then, "I didn't understand what it would mean for the farm at all."

That said, if you can choose whether you'll become a parent during a chaotic time of life or a more stable one, aiming for the time of stability can make everything easier. That's because kids, and especially babies, bring their own unpredictable chaos and will necessarily take time and energy away from literally every other thing in your life: your farm or homestead, your relationships, other work, your own care. Time available for work will be compressed into new units of time based around naps, childcare, and parenting duties.

CAN YOU TIME A BABY'S ARRIVAL?

Knowing that babies can disrupt life and work, some farmers aim their pregnancies to correspond with lulls in seasonal work. We did that, and it worked quite well with our first child. I got pregnant in March and went into labor the evening after our final December CSA delivery. We enjoyed several weeks of quiet time for bonding with our baby without a large farm workload.

Jordan Goldsmith said she and her wife, Melissa, had similar goals: "We chose only to try and get pregnant in months that would lead us to a fall or early-winter birth. We wanted to take the time to figure out how to be parents without the pressure of the season." Many farmers I spoke with shared similar sentiments about trying to avoid the primary growing season or lambing or other work-heavy times. Farmers who have been pregnant before and have a better understanding of how the pregnancy experience is likely to go for them sometimes also consider other challenges—such as what time of year they might want to deal with early nausea.

If you want to plan the timing of a birth, it's helpful to learn about fertility cycles well in advance. *Taking Charge of Your Fertility: The Definitive Guide to Natural Birth Control, Pregnancy Achievement, and Reproductive Health* by Toni Weschler is a comprehensive guide to the ins and outs of a menstrual and ovulation cycle, including how to carefully track cycles and fertility windows based on physical indicators. Once you determine whether there's an ideal time of year to plan a birth, count back about 10 months to find the ideal timing for conception. It's helpful to set a goal of a *range* of months when it might work well to have a baby since conception can take multiple cycles or longer to achieve.

THERE ARE LIMITS TO PLANNING

Clearly, we can only plan so much. Pregnancy and birth are biological processes with many variables not in our control. Just as we know each growing season may have unpredictable complications, conception, pregnancy, and birth can also come with challenges. Many farmers I spoke with shared stories of pregnancy loss or difficulties with fertility. In those cases, trying to carefully plan birth timing became less important than simply the goal of becoming parents.

Sometimes pregnancy itself comes as a surprise. Tara Chapman of Two Hives Honey in Texas was not planning to ever have children. Her life already seemed very full. She told her fiancé her plans before they were married. "I don't see how a baby fits into my life," she told him. "I am almost 40. I work incredibly long hours, and my business is everything." But then, early in 2021, she became pregnant. "This was 100 percent not planned," she said. In her case, though she hadn't

> *"Make sure you can be completely missing from your farm and it will still keep going. Even plan to take a full year off your farm if you can financially figure that out."*
>
> —JORDAN GOLDSMITH

planned the timing (much less the pregnancy!), it worked out well with her work with her hives and business.

Hanako Myers and Marko Colby had even less notice of the actual date they'd become parents. They were on a waiting list for an open adoption for almost two years. Meanwhile, they were busy running Midori Farm in Washington. "Every day was a day where we could have gotten a phone call and then been parents by the end of the night," Hanako said, adding that almost every day on their farm has an intense and demanding workload. "But we knew that when the call came, everything else was going to have to go on the back burner." They finally got the call on the last day of June 2020. "We had about 40 hours' notice from the time we learned we were going to meet our son to when we met him," she said. "He's been with us ever since."

1 You can't anticipate the experience.

Aside from people who grew up in large families, most farmer-parents echo the sentiments of new parents in general: surprise at how total the changes are in one's life upon becoming a parent. "Nothing that anyone else tells you can prepare you for it," Katrina McQuail said. "People shared the most wonderful experiences and advice with us, and yet nothing could have prepared us for it."

2 Parenting never stops.

Jordan Goldsmith of Moonrose Farm in Massachusetts said that before becoming a parent, she didn't fully realize how all-encompassing parenting is. "What I didn't realize was the 'constant-ness' of it," she said. "Never being alone or never having the solo time to complete a task is challenging."

3 It's vital to seek balance.

Now that he has three children, John McCafferty said that he has a lot more perspective on how parenting can fit into a life. "With the first child, you're overwhelmed with this joyous responsibility and you give it everything you've got," he said. "But now I know that I've got to find energy from other sources as well. Part of that's friends and part of that's work. And then I have more energy to be the parent as well."

4 Life will be magnified in every direction.

"Both farming and parenthood are labors of love," said Katrina. "They're very rewarding, but also you can have horrible days or moments. When you combine them, you get even greater highs, but also potentially lower lows."

5 It gets easier.

John (and many, many other farmer-parents) said that parenting gets easier in many ways as kids grow older and more independent and capable. "These stages will pass," he said, "and things get easier."

"I was at a farmer gathering and I asked, 'Farming and kids—how does this work? People, tell me!' Everyone just laughed, and I thought, 'Oh, that's not a good sign.' Afterward, someone offered this advice: 'If you want to farm and you want to have kids, just do it. There's no perfect time. Everyone figures it out.'"

—AMY FRYE

PLAN TO BE FLEXIBLE

When preparing to become parents, it's important to make room in your life and on your farm for the big changes ahead—as much as possible, anyway. Casey and I knew that I was going to step back from doing physical work on the farm for some undetermined period after our first child was born, so we figured we either needed to cut back on our farm's work or bring on extra hands. We ended up doing both—we decided to discontinue our farmers' market sales and focus on growing our popular CSA program, and we also hired our first employees while I was pregnant.

Of course, making these changes cost us money, and we had to account for that in our farm and household budget. It forced us to rethink the structure and scale of our farm for a few years to accommodate for my missing labor. It was a profound change on many levels, as I'll address in later chapters. But having a plan of some kind is essential, because becoming parents changes everything.

While you're developing a plan, you'll also need to (perhaps paradoxically) prepare yourself to be more flexible than ever before. Between pregnancy, birth, and early parenting, there are so many opportunities to have unexpected challenges. Amy Frye of Boldly Grown Farm in Washington thinks farming helps with growing that mindset. "Assume you don't know how anything will unfold," she said about becoming a parent. "I feel like farming is good experience for parenting because you're used to being flexible and not knowing what the season is going to hold."

Even then, expect the adjustment to exceed even farming expectations for flexibility. Jordan Goldsmith of Moonrose Farm had a particularly challenging pregnancy and slow birth recovery, requiring her to quickly and radically shift her relationship to the farm. Based on her experience, she wants other farmers to at least be aware that things could be very tough. "Honestly, although my pregnancy was rough," she said, "it wasn't as bad as some people have. And you don't get to choose your pregnancy experience. I'm kind of a control-freak type of person with the business, and I want to do as much as we can without killing ourselves. But I had to give up so much control that year. And I think it was good for me. I had let go of expectations of things being perfect." Her farm also took practical measures to account for the shift in her ability to work. "We used a lot more plastic [mulch for weed prevention] than normal that year to try to get ahead of things."

CAN YOU TAKE PARENTAL LEAVE?

In addition to (perhaps) timing the arrival of a new child for a slower time of year, some farmers can take actual parental leave or step back from farming for several months. In my conversations with farmers, I found this was more likely for farmers who had many people involved with their farm—a farm partner, co-owners, or long-term employees— or who were employees themselves.

Elise Bortz started planning for having children years before she got pregnant because she knew she wanted to be a parent *and* she wanted her farm business to continue to thrive. She brought an employee on as a business partner at Elysian Fields Farm in North Carolina, which allowed her to take several months off after each of her children was born. As employees at Soul Fire Farm, a nonprofit farm in New York, Brooke Bridges and her husband, Kai Thomas, were able to take 12 full weeks of paid parental leave because of their state's policies and their employer's flexibility.

Emily Board and Dan Brisebois are both co-owners and employees of Tourne-Sol Cooperative Farm in Quebec. They started the farm with three other farmers in 2004, and now there are 10 co-owners. Because they are also employees, the owners are all able to make use of the parental leave provided in Quebec, which between two parents can add up to almost an entire year of partially paid leave.

The farm itself still needs to prepare for the absence of owners, something the Tourne-Sol team has learned how to do over its 20 years. "We built a farm that offers flexibility in our schedules," Dan said. "Not everybody's working in a given year, but enough people are that the work can get done. And we'll hire and compensate for that, too." All 10 owners are parents at this point, so the farm has been through the process many times. "We know what you can drop and that there are certain times of year that are going to be harder than other times of year," Dan said. "But, because we've done this so long, we also know it passes."

THE REAL REASONS WE BECOME PARENTS

Ultimately, the decision to have children and become a parent isn't about whether your farm is financially viable yet or whether you have enough employees or whether you can finesse the perfect timing. The question is whether you feel called to do the work of raising the next generation of humans and all that entails.

For us and many other farmers, knowing that becoming a parent would likely complicate our farming life didn't matter—kids were worth the costs to our business. I'm assuming that since you're reading this book, you're probably leaning the same way. I hope that in these pages and stories you find information to help you navigate that journey but remember that you'll learn as you go. You can't and don't need to have it all figured out before taking the first steps.

DISCUSSION AND JOURNALING QUESTIONS

▶ *If you're farming and/or homesteading but don't have children yet, what are your thoughts and feelings about becoming a parent?*

▶ *What processes or infrastructure might you want to have in place before becoming a parent? What's a reasonable time frame for meeting those goals?*

▶ *If your plans for becoming a parent don't go as expected, what resources can you pull on to help you navigate disappointments or unexpected challenges?*

▶ *What parts of your farm or homestead operation can be simplified (temporarily or permanently) to make extra space for adjusting to family life? Whom can you ask for help with your transition?*

PREGNANCY, BIRTH, AND POSTPARTUM HEALING

I LEARNED I WAS PREGNANT with our first child on an early-spring day. As I looked at the positive pregnancy test, I realized that this next adventure would be something Casey and I would do together—but *my* body would bear the brunt of the unpredictability of pregnancy. How would being pregnant affect our coming farming season? How would it affect my ability to work at my very physical job and contribute to our growing small business and livelihood?

Books and resources abound to help people understand "what to expect" during pregnancy, but, of course, one of the first things most people learn when researching pregnancy is how different the experience is for different people. While certain elements are common to most pregnancies, few are applicable to everyone, and the severity of challenges can vary widely. Even for an individual, each pregnancy is likely to be different from any other they may have had before.

Farmers are no exception to these rules. Each pregnancy is its own experience; each can bring different symptoms and limitations. The good news is that most farmers told me they were able to work through their pregnancies, albeit with accommodations and often with a lot more rest outside of work hours than they previously needed.

ACCOMMODATING PREGNANCY CHALLENGES

For most farmers, the biggest early challenges were classics for pregnant people everywhere: fatigue and sometimes nausea. Tory Shelley, who works at Featherbed Lane Farm in New York, experienced both. She said that she was grateful to be farming during her first trimester. "It was really great to be outside," she said. "Having something like harvesting or transplanting focuses you. You're just doing this repetitive motion. Instead of focusing on feeling icky, I told myself, 'Just do the thing. Just do the thing.'"

While she never actually threw up from early nausea, she was glad to be in an outside space where that would have been easy to do. "I wouldn't have to go find a bathroom," she noted. She kept snacks with her and ate while she worked, something her crew doesn't normally do. "Those little changes were really important."

The fatigue mostly affected her time outside of work. "I went home at the end of the day and slept," she said. "So my work didn't suffer so much from me being tired—it was the rest of my life. I came home and literally just took naps and ate boiled eggs."

Sarah Kostyu of K7 Farm in Michigan has 10 children. Her pregnancies were healthy, she said, and allowed her to continue working through them. She has a five-acre garden she tends with help from her family. "I have put the garden in right up to going into labor," she said. "I've worked straight through our gardening season while pregnant."

Even so, Sarah said, pregnancy is still something to navigate: "It definitely slows me down." When we spoke, her most recent pregnancy had given her morning sickness for several months during planting season. "We did have a lower yield of potatoes and corn

"*I was pregnant with my third child here at Wingspan, and it was such an incredible experience—my healthiest pregnancy and easiest labor. I think it was from being outside during my pregnancy and gardening in safe ways.*"

—ALYSON LARKIN

because weeds took over," she said. "It was a struggle to reclaim things once I was feeling better, but I just moved forward one step at a time and tried to prioritize what needed to happen."

For most people, any nausea and fatigue decrease about midway through pregnancy, just as the body mechanics of a growing belly and other symptoms become more of a concern. While many pregnant farmers continue to be very productive up until just before birth, they often require accommodations.

I worked until the day I went into labor, but I made changes along the way. For example, I still harvested, but I no longer carried the heaviest bins when we were in the fields. I had to communicate clearly with my husband and our employees so that I could continue working (something that I wanted to do and that felt good) while making sure they understood how my body was rapidly changing. That kind of communication isn't always easy, and it's important for coworkers and partners to initiate conversations, pay attention, and listen carefully, too.

Katrina McQuail, who operates Meeting Place Organic Farm in Ontario with her parents and employees, found it interesting to observe the way her body changed during her pregnancies. "The loosening of the ligaments in my pelvis meant that certain movements and actions were harder or more painful than I expected," she said. "Also, our farm has beautiful rolling hills that winded me quickly when I was pregnant."

She accommodated the changes by working more slowly and accepting that there were tasks she needed to hand off to other people on the farm. Katrina had experienced pregnancy losses and found herself wanting to be very careful around the farm's animals, including their draft horses. "I was so afraid of something happening and me losing the pregnancies that it meant everyone else had to work with the animals."

"I learned to listen to my body and pay more attention to it; to remind myself it was working really hard even if I didn't feel like it was doing work that I could see."

—KRISTINA McQUAIL

5 COMFY CLOTHING
OPTIONS FOR PREGNANT FARMERS

1 Overalls and coveralls

I worked in overalls during both of my pregnancies. I unbuttoned a pair of normal overalls until they no longer fit and then switched to secondhand pregnancy-specific overalls. Tara Chapman of Two Hives Honey in Texas wore size XXL men's coveralls—they were loose enough that they didn't sit right on her skin, which helped prevent stings through her clothing.

2 Adapted or inexpensive outerwear

My fisherman-style workwear rain bibs and jacket fit through my whole pregnancy. Some farmers adapt existing gear by buying zip-in extensions to make room for their growing bellies. Tory Shelley, who works at Featherbed Lane Farm in New York, bought a plastic poncho-style raincoat. "I saw in the picture the person was wearing it with a backpack," she said. "I thought, 'That will fit around my belly.' It did."

3 Leggings and stretchy exercise clothing

Pregnancy-specific leggings and stretchy exercise gear are also popular options for farmers because of the ease of full movement they provide for working in the fields. Leggings can be paired with gardening-style kneepads to prevent ripping holes while kneeling in soft pants.

4 Lightweight layers

Pregnancy itself can increase sensitivity to heat, so it's important to dress in looser and lighter clothing that allows you to stay as cool as possible when it's hot. Pregnancy can affect skin's light sensitivity, so be sure to also wear sunscreen and a hat.

5 Supportive undergarments

Some farmers find wearing supportive pregnancy belly bands or undergarments is helpful when moving vigorously in the fields. Likewise, many farmers wear compression socks to help prevent swelling in the feet and ankles after a day of working and standing.

PREGNANCY TIPS FROM A MIDWIFE

Even a healthy pregnancy changes a person's body and needs. Staying strong is important for the physical health of the parent and baby as well as for preparing for birth and recovery. So, it's important for a pregnant farmer to listen to their care provider *and* their body as they continue to work and farm.

Ideally, choose a midwife or doctor who understands your physical job and can help support your goals while keeping in mind your overall health and any specific needs. Oregon midwife Jen Holland, CPM, has worked with many farmers and homesteaders over the course of her career. She said she finds most farmers to be very physically fit and well nourished, both important starts for a healthy pregnancy and birth.

Rather than restricting activity, Jen works with farmers to help them learn new body mechanics and to listen to their bodies for feedback about how familiar activities might change over the course of their pregnancy. Here are some of Jen's primary safety and health tips for pregnant farmers.

Listen to your body!

Watch for red flags while doing physical work. Danger signs include preterm labor, the uterus being more "active" than it should be (i.e., cramping), and bleeding or loss of fluid. Watch out for any strong pain. You shouldn't be in pain.

If you are in doubt about any symptoms or feelings, ease off on the activity, rest, and contact your care provider.

Focus on body alignment.

Support your body while doing your work. Put your weight over your heels rather than on your toes to ensure that the large muscles at the back of your body (glutes, hamstrings, back muscles) are supporting your body weight, rather than adding strain to the belly and pelvic floor. Exhaling with exertion helps shift the load to those bigger muscles and off the pelvic floor.

Find moments during the day to take long, slow belly breaths and bring your awareness to your body. Feel for places in your body where you're clenching, especially the butt or pelvic floor. Work on relaxing all those clenched muscles.

Stay hydrated.

The standard recommendation is that pregnant people drink half their weight in ounces during the day; a 160-pound person should aim to drink at least 80 ounces of water per day. On hot days or during periods of heavy exertion, farmers need to drink more—and consider adding electrolytes to water—to avoid dehydration.

Consider pelvic floor physical therapy.

Physically active people often have tight pelvic muscles, which can create challenges in labor and postpartum healing. Seek pelvic floor physical therapy during pregnancy if you experience symptoms of hypertonic (tight) pelvic floor muscles, including painful sex, pain in the pelvis, history of very painful cramping with periods, or

incontinence. Don't wait for more problems before getting therapy.

Plan for postpartum rest.

After birth, try to rest *in bed* for two weeks. Jen told me busy farmers usually laugh at this advice, but this rest time is critical for pelvic floor recovery, bonding with the baby, preventing postpartum mood disorders, and building a milk supply.

It's okay to be creative about finding places to rest—for example, spending time on a blanket under a tree or in a hammock on a porch. But focus on lying down, resting, healing, and bonding.

After that time of rest, ease back into work slowly, keeping in mind your body's work of healing from pregnancy and birth and adjusting to the work of caring for a baby.

DON'T PUSH PAST PAIN

Tara Chapman of Two Hives Honey in Texas worked until she was 38 weeks pregnant. The latter part of her pregnancy coincided with the heat of the Texas summer and the honey harvest. Though pregnancy hadn't been particularly comfortable for her, up until that point, she had been able to do most of the bee work and didn't think much about making accommodations for herself. One day, the temperature rose above 100°F (38°C). She kept on lifting boxes. "I had been doing everything that I would've done otherwise up until that point," she said. "So I got a little overconfident, and then my overconfidence hit a real tough, long day, and I didn't have enough water with me." She got dehydrated and experienced severe cramping, making her realize she was pushing too hard.

It was a reminder that even though she was a strong farmer, the pregnancy had changed her body and she needed to be more careful. "When you work in agriculture, your bar for what you can deal with is so much higher than the average person because we work in all conditions. I get stung by bees for a living. It's not unusual for me to take two dozen stings in a week. So my tolerance for pain is high." Tara had to learn to listen to her body's signals in a different way for the rest of the pregnancy.

THE BEAUTY OF FARMING WHILE PREGNANT

While it can be hard and exhausting and just plain *different* to farm while pregnant, for many farmers it can also be a beautiful time. I had been farming for five years when I became pregnant, and I remember feeling more connected to the natural world than ever before. I had been closely involved in the work of growing plants, and now I was experiencing similar forces at work in my own body.

Brooke Bridges felt similar awe and wonder as she farmed at Soul Fire Farm in New York while pregnant with her first child. "I worked the entire pregnancy, packing for the CSA every week," she said. "There was something so magical for me to be growing this little seed in my body and planting little seedlings at the same time. It was almost like she was planting the sustenance with me. It was really a beautiful experience, and I feel so lucky to have been able to do that with her."

It isn't always beautiful, however. Brooke's second pregnancy was different. "It was a much harder pregnancy," she said. "I was really sick at the beginning—I lost 15 pounds." At the same time, she was tending to and breastfeeding a toddler, and also farming. "I was so drained," she remembered.

Soul Fire Farm ended up having to bring in extra labor to accommodate the shift in what Brooke was able to do. "I could do the easier things like greenhouse seeding, but not a lot of weeding or heavy-duty mulching or transplanting," she said. "At a certain point, it just got to be too much being out there all day in the hot sun and losing fluids and calories that I didn't really have to give. I focused a lot more on the administrative side of things this past year."

Brooke's experience is a good reminder that even for people who have already farmed while pregnant, subsequent pregnancies can bring unexpected and new experiences, especially if now they're managing pregnancy *and* older children.

During my second pregnancy, I felt physically better than in my first, but managing a toddler and doing physical farm work was an entirely different load. I couldn't rest whenever I needed to, and it was ultimately easier for me to pass the physical work of our farm on to Casey and our employees and focus on administrative tasks that I could do during nap times and when I had a babysitter.

Christina Menchini had a similar experience with her second pregnancy. With her first pregnancy, she and her husband were just starting Campfire Farms in Oregon, and it felt essential that she be as involved as possible. "My first year of farming I was pregnant, and I just decided that I was going to be the one who doesn't miss a beat," Christina said. But things were very different a few years later when she got pregnant again: "I had a hard pregnancy, physically and mentally. It was really challenging that I couldn't just power through it, because I've been able to power through everything." Ultimately she couldn't do much physical farm work at all. "I was nauseated for seven months and trying to work and dealing with vertigo," she said. "It was a hard blow to the ego feeling like I wasn't pulling my weight on the farm."

PREPARING FOR BIRTH

As I prepared for my first birth, I found myself wondering whether all my farming experience would help me in some way. I'd hoped that being physically active would somehow translate to having an easier birth, but, of course, I had no way to know whether that would be true. Like pregnancy, birth is a mysterious and often unpredictable physical process. The farmers I spoke with reported a wide range of experiences with birth, ranging from straightforward, unmedicated births to C-sections. Some people felt great within days of giving birth; others took weeks or months to recover even a basic feeling of wellness.

Tara Chapman felt like farming helped her prepare for the challenge of birth: "For me, farming instills a certain resiliency that you

The BEST THING about FAMILY FARMING is...
Seeing my kids working in the garden. Knowing they have at least a little piece of the homesteading I experienced as a kid makes my heart sing. KRISTIN POOL COHEN, SUPER HOUSE

just can't get any other way, both physically and mentally." Katrina McQuail agreed: "Witnessing countless animals give birth allowed me to be open to all the possibilities that the birth experience could entail. From horses to pigs to cattle to goats, sheep, and bunnies, each species is unique, and each time is unique. I knew it would be the same for me."

The one certainty of birth is that it radically disrupts your life. Even if a farmer has been working right up until labor begins, at that moment they (and their partner) will need to put down everything to focus on one of the most profound passages and physical challenges of a person's life. And that experience will be followed by an intense period of rest, recovery, and adjustment to the entirely new reality of parenting a newborn.

It's essential to have farm plans in place for birth's disruptions. My second child was due during the farming season, so in the lead-up to my due date, Casey and I worked with our employees to make lists and plans with explicit directions for every possibility. We didn't know whether I'd go into labor on a delivery day or a fieldwork day, and we wanted to make sure our employees knew what to do in any circumstance. With both pregnancies, we also let our customers know what to expect, as we cut back slightly on some commitments, such as restaurant sales, in the period after birth.

ASK FOR SUPPORT AND HELP

It's also essential to make plans for support for the new parent(s)! Katrina McQuail had a farmer friend who had her baby on a Sunday, after a 24-hour labor, and then was back in the field on Wednesday for harvesting. "Her story inspired me to ask my parents for at least up to six weeks of help," Katrina said.

Even if they've carefully planned parental leave (see Chapter 7), many farmers will find that their farm and household (and potentially older children) still need some attention and support immediately after birth. Don't hesitate to ask other people to help as much as possible with meals, farm chores, and childcare for older children. Jordan Goldsmith and her wife, Melissa, had help with meals after the birth of their daughter. "We're grateful to have some really good cooks in our life, and we got spoiled by having good, nutritious food to sustain us for several weeks after having the baby," she said. "Having that plan in place ahead was great." There are websites and apps that can help people coordinate and communicate about helping with meals.

Brooke Bridges said that the Soul Fire Farm community chipped in around both her births to help support her and her husband. "Our neighbors asked if they could clean the house for us before we came back from the hospital. So, we came home to a clean space," she said. "When we had our second child, in the first couple of weeks people signed up for time slots to take our toddler out on walks."

DON'T DOWNPLAY POSTPARTUM HEALING

The time just after the birth is an important one for healing and adjusting to life with a newborn. For many, slowly restarting physical work can feel like a welcome return to normal, and the process flows smoothly as they take on more and more of their usual tasks over the weeks and months following birth.

Elise Bortz of Elysian Fields Farm in North Carolina planned carefully to take a three-month maternity leave with each of her kids. For her that ended up being very necessary. "I had to have an emergency C-section," she said. "You can't predict that, and it's a major surgery. You have to be careful afterward. They won't even let you drive for three weeks." And the full recovery from a C-section takes much longer, especially for farmers hoping to lift and bend again.

Tara Chapman said she didn't realize what this period would be like and had expected to get back to lighter kinds of work quickly. "I gave birth on October 14, and a week later I had a hive tour on the calendar that I thought I was going to do," she told me. "I did not plan for anyone else to do it because it didn't occur to me that I couldn't be out there. So, I did it. It was traumatic. And then I went back to bed for a week because I started bleeding again, and I bled for another 10 days because I really screwed up my pelvic floor."

Though work can feel urgent, it's important to remember how unique this postpartum time of life is. For a first-time parent, it is a period of profound changes and adjustments. Even people who have multiple children will still have only a few weeks to know each of them as newborns. Making as much space as possible in your life to be present, rest, and bond with your baby can help turn a potentially stressful time into a sweet passage. You, your partner, and any other family members are all becoming new people as you get to know the new human in your life.

DISCUSSION AND JOURNALING QUESTIONS

▶ *If you are pregnant now, how are you feeling? What have been the joys in your experience? What challenges have you dealt with so far? What are your fears, concerns, or hopes for the remainder of your pregnancy?*

▶ *If you are postpartum, how are your healing and adjusting going? What kind of support are you receiving or do you still need? Whom can you ask to help?*

▶ *If you have been pregnant in the past, what were the highlights of the experience? What challenges did you have to address, and what resources helped you through?*

CHAPTER

9

Brooke Bridges and Kai Thomas
Soul Fire Farm
Grafton, New York

A BABY
ON THE
FARM

ABOUT A WEEK AFTER OUR FIRST CHILD, Rusty, was born, my husband and I were sitting in our living room. I was still awkwardly working to get Rusty latched so that he could nurse, and my husband was helping as much as possible and then bringing me water and snacks as needed. I watched Rusty as he fed and then slowly fell asleep on the big nursing pillow in my lap. I had been sitting or lying down all week, and every waking (and drowsing!) hour had been centered on the most basic activities: nursing, burping, diaper changes, cleaning around his healing belly button . . . life felt like a weird, very slow, small but endless emergency as we learned how to respond to Rusty's cues and take care of such a vulnerable and fragile-feeling new life. Each time it seemed that we resolved one need, another one arose. And he slept only for an hour or two at a time, even overnight.

There was deep sweetness in this at-home mundane baby work, but in that moment all the changes in our life suddenly seemed to hit me emotionally. It was so fundamentally different from the life I'd led just a week and a half before, when I was still harvesting and going to

Katrina McQuail holds her newborn in her farmhouse.

town and interacting with customers. Tears streamed down my face as I looked over at Casey and asked, "Is this what our life is now? Are we just going to sit here at home and not move except to wipe faces and bums?"

Of course, we were eventually able to do more than just sit around the house, but I was correct that our life was forever changed. No longer would we be able to plan a single moment of our day without considering the needs of our child and making sure that someone was available to care for him. But aside from addressing childcare needs (see Chapter 10), we also had to transition to our new roles as parents and deal with all the special challenges that come in the first year or two of a baby's life.

WHAT CAN YOU DO WITH A NEWBORN?

Unless you have much younger siblings or have provided childcare for babies, it may be hard to understand the incessant needs of babies and toddlers. And babies are born with their temperaments pretty well established. I've certainly known farmers who were able to ease into their parenting life by successfully planning a birth for a slow time of year, giving themselves plenty of space to adjust, and having a baby with a chill temperament or good sleep habits. Alas, most of the time, our experience with our babies depends on factors beyond our control.

Before having her son, Tara Chapman of Two Hives Honey said she had some sense that her work would be limited, but not to the extent she experienced. "I'd planned for the bee work to be covered, but what didn't occur to me is I couldn't just do everything else: I couldn't just get up and answer emails and direct staff and show up to an event and direct people on where to go and what to do," she said. "I didn't account for the fact that I would not have the mental capacity, the sleep, or the time."

After six weeks off, Tory Shelley began bringing her baby with her to work at Featherbed Lane Farm in New York. Her employer is also a good friend who was already a parent and understood that she'd need accommodation on the job. "I just stayed longer if I was nursing her for half an hour or something," Tory said. She also cut back her hours to part-time, and the farm hired another year-round employee.

Even with those adjustments, Tory found that working with her baby was incredibly difficult, sometimes in surprising ways. Sleep deprivation was hard, but she also found herself continually frustrated by trying to meet competing needs between her newborn daughter and her work. "I'd be washing lettuce in the greenhouse and she would wake up

"I was traumatized by those first four to five months of my son's life because I didn't prepare. Nobody told me, and I didn't know to ask for help."

—TARA CHAPMAN

and want milk," Tory said. "It'd be 80 degrees, the lettuce is wilting, but my baby's crying." Her employer was supportive and tried to send other employees to help when needed, but Tory still found the situations stressful. "What's really more important here?" she'd ask herself. "The high standards I used to hold for my job mean nothing because my baby is crying. So, why am I here if I'm not doing my farm work?"

Tory said she's glad her daughter spent so much time outside in her early months, but she would not do it that way again. "I think you need to take that time off or be really comfortable giving someone else your newborn," she said. "Those are the choices." (See Chapter 7 for more about planning parental leave.)

Christina Menchini of Campfire Farms in Oregon had a similar experience adjusting to a new role. "With my first, I was trying to figure out whether I can be a mama with a baby in a sling at the farmers' market. And I found my kid is not into this whatsoever," she said. "So, no, I can't be that." She said it was hard to realize how often she was going to have to ask for support to do jobs that were easy before. This was especially true because she was nursing, making her the default primary parent. "If I'm going to be at the market, what kind of support do I need and who does the support have to come from?" she said. "It

"Being a parent took most of my time and energy in the first year. My wife, Melissa, did more of the farming. I still did all the planning and the daily list, mostly over FaceTime, but she was executing it with the help of our manager."

—JORDAN GOLDSMITH

was so hard for me to ask for help. It felt like a weakness or a failure every time."

For a couple with a newborn, if one parent is clearly the primary caregiver (such as if one is nursing), it is important for the other parent to try to anticipate needs and meet them before being asked. That process can require lots of communication, some of which might feel painful. But be sure to check in with each other regularly about how each of you is doing with your load and what each of you needs. It's very likely you both will have unmet needs in the early days of parenthood, because so much energy goes into meeting the needs of the baby—and this is true for all parents, not just farmer-parents. John Gottman and Julie Schwartz Gottman have an excellent book about the challenges relationships face after having a baby: *And Baby Makes Three: The Six-Step Plan for Preserving Marital Intimacy and Rekindling Romance After Baby Arrives.*

WILL I EVER SLEEP THROUGH THE NIGHT AGAIN?

Sleep deprivation is a challenge that all parents face in the early days of parenting. There are those rare babies who sleep through the night early on, and their parents can skip much of the information in this section. But the vast majority of parents will experience several months (or even years) of interrupted sleep, which can affect every part of life.

Jordan Goldsmith was surprised at how deeply the lost sleep impacted everything. "I was able to sustain what I was doing before having a kid by having uninterrupted rest," she said. "I didn't realize how important it was for me to get really solid long nights of sleep and how much not having that sleep would affect and impact my happiness . . . and lead to not being able to concentrate and finish a thought."

WORKING WITH A BABY IN A CARRIER

Carriers and wraps are invaluable tools for people caring for babies. Babies often enjoy the comfort of being close to an adult and the motion of being walked around, plus carriers allow the adult to have their hands free to do tasks.

But there are limits to what kind of work can and should be done while wearing your baby. Many farmers I spoke with said that before having children, they imagined doing their same job but with a baby strapped to their back. Most reported that the reality was more limited than they expected, both for logistical and safety reasons. Here are some important guidelines for working with a baby in a carrier, many of which also apply to working with a baby or child nearby in a stroller.

Use it correctly.

Read your carrier's instructions, watch videos, and practice in low-stakes situations before working with a baby in a carrier. Proper body positioning matters for all babies and toddlers, but be especially aware of not constricting airways or covering faces of newborns by not letting them slump or be curled up, as can happen in a sling. Also pay attention to your baby's temperature so that they don't overheat. For more safety guidelines about baby wearing, visit the Carrying Matters website. (See Suggested Reading and Other Resources, page 222.)

Be aware of risks.

Consider whether your task poses risks to your baby. Watch for flying objects (for example, splattered mud from washing) or items your baby might grab. Is it cold or hot out? Do you need to provide protection from sun or biting insects?

Some kinds of farm work should not be done while you are caring for a child (see Chapter 10). Do not wear a baby or child while:

- Using machinery
- Working with large or aggressive animals
- Applying chemical pesticides or fertilizers to crops
- Working on ladders

Listen to your body.

When deciding whether to wear your baby while working, consider your own body mechanics, your comfort in the carrier, and child placement (chest, hip, or back). Work requiring bending over for long periods of time can put extra strain on your core if you are also wearing a baby. Your baby will grow quickly and become heavier, so stay aware of changes in your comfort.

Listen to your baby.

Always stay aware of your baby's communication cues. Be aware of how *your* motions might create discomfort for them. For example, our children squirmed and fussed when we tried to do work bending over. Watch for all the usual baby signs that might indicate a pressing physical need such as for food or a diaper change.

When you have a baby with you, whether you are wearing them or not, you must continue to care for the baby while you are working, even if this means interrupting your task. You may not be able to finish your task, so have a backup plan or another person available to help if you need to step away. One bonus: Many babies sleep well in carriers, so many farmers overlap work time with nap time.

Wear your baby for low-intensity, upright tasks.

Despite all these warnings, there are many tasks on a farm or homestead that are well suited to doing while wearing babies and toddlers. Casey and I found we had the best success with simple, repetitive tasks that involved moving around in a mostly upright position.

Tasks that worked for us and for other farmers

- Walking fields to assess farm plans and check on crops
- Holding farm meetings and giving instructions to workers
- Harvesting mostly upright (picking trellised peas, apples, raspberries, etc.)
- Using a push-seeder to sow crops
- Doing farm cleanup tasks
- Pruning orchard trees or thinning fruit (not on a ladder)
- Selling at market
- Doing nonhazardous animal chores (feeding, collecting eggs, etc.)
- Moving portable fencing

Hanako Myers told me that sleep deprivation blurred her and Marko's memory of any farm work that took place during their son's first year of life. "Staff who were with us that summer will say, 'Hey, remember that onion crop in the fall of 2020—remember what happened with that?' And we're like, 'No, we cannot remember anything.'" Like many new parents, some moments stand out through the fog. "We remember everything about our son and what it was like to have a baby," she said. "But on the farm side of it, we were just kind of swimming through it, just robots or something."

DEALING WITH POSTPARTUM DEPRESSION

Sleep deprivation along with with hormone shifts and identity changes can all combine to trigger postpartum depression. According to CDC research, about one in eight postpartum individuals will experience postpartum depression, and more experience the "baby blues," a less severe version. I experienced the baby blues with both of my children and also a strong increase in anxiety for several years. In my case, time and (eventually) more sleep helped me feel normal again. But some farmer-parents will need more help.

Amy Frye of Boldly Grown Farm said it took her a year to recognize her postpartum depression, and her husband actually noticed it first. "In hindsight, it seems silly," she said. "I'm a pretty smart person. I should have been more aware of it. But I thought, 'I don't feel depressed. I don't feel sad.' My main symptoms ranged from intense irritability to rage, which I didn't associate with depression." Amy was able to treat her depression with a combination of medication, therapy, exercise, and other self-care tools. When it occurred after her second child was born, she was able to recognize it more quickly with her therapist's help. (See Chapter 6 for more tips about addressing stress and mental health on the farm.)

ADAPTING TO EVOLVING IDENTITIES

There's no avoiding the emotional transition that comes to parents during the adjustment. New identities, roles, and life rhythms are being born, and there is some grief that comes with saying goodbye to the life we lived before—and, for farmers, seeing our relationship to the farm change. I remember many tearful conversations with Casey in the early months of parenting, and I don't think we could have avoided all those hard emotions. They were part of the process.

Dan Brisebois and Emily Board of Tourne-Sol Cooperative Farm in Quebec both took parental leave when their three children were babies. They found that they had to rearrange their priorities and identities after becoming parents, especially as they realized it was impossible for both of them to work full-time on the farm in the way they had before having kids.

Dan took on the role of being the more flexible parent who could be available for driving kids to childcare and school and be on call for emergencies. "We put family first, farm second, and then other stuff after," said Dan. "Sometimes being a farmer, especially a young farmer starting your own business, becomes who you are and you have to do it a certain way. Realizing that farming is just an aspect of what I do has made it easier for me—farming doesn't completely define my success."

5 SIMPLE STRATEGIES
FOR COPING WITH EXHAUSTION

1 Make lists.

In the depths of sleep deprivation, John McCafferty said making lists was essential. He made them before going to bed. "If you've already arranged the next day," he said, "you don't need to stress about it." John said it helps to make those lists very specific. Including small concrete tasks that can be done in brief moments of attention can help increase productivity (or sometimes even just the happy feeling of completion). "You get a little boost from being able to tick off something," he noted.

2 Carve out brief rests.

Jordan Goldsmith said that before having a child, she often took a shower and then lay down for 20 minutes after a day of farm work. "That's just nonexistent in my life anymore," she said. But she and her wife do aim to provide each other with midafternoon breaks from both farming and parenting. "Having a little bit of a break after work, even if it's 20 minutes, makes a huge difference for my happiness and attention span before shifting back into parenting for the evening," Jordan said.

Parents will think about their children's sleep habits and how they affect work and their own sleep quality for many years.

3 Be honest about your capacity for work.

Jordan also said she tries to have realistic expectations for herself when sleep deprivation is at its worst. "You're just not going to get as much done when you are tired. You don't have the physical or mental ability," she said. When she's extremely tired, she communicates that fact to her employees. "Be real with your crew, too," she advised. "We have an incredible crew of people, so they're very understanding. It's nice to be able to say, 'Last night we didn't get any sleep, so I might not make any sense, and we'll figure it out together.'"

4 Share nighttime duties.

After experiencing sleep deprivation during their first child's babyhood, Amy Frye and her husband decided to come up with strategies for sharing the load after their second child was born. They hired a night doula to come a few times to take care of their baby so they could just sleep and be more rested for their full-time farm work. Beyond that, the two parents split nighttime duties, with Jacob doing the first feeding with pumped milk so that Amy could have a longer stretch of uninterrupted sleep before she woke to nurse later in the night.

5 Caffeinate!

In the early days of parenthood, Casey and I both embraced a daily cup of coffee as part of our sleep deprivation survival plan. I later switched to decaf (and then no coffee at all) as our children grew and I returned to getting consistent uninterrupted sleep. Obviously, people's bodies and reactions to caffeine vary, but a lot of farmer-parents express deep gratitude for their morning cup of coffee or tea. "Coffee is essential to parenthood," said Jordan. "We don't even drink that much, but without it I don't know that we could be humans."

WHEN IT'S BABY #2 (OR 3 OR 4 . . .)

Brooke Bridges brought her first baby with her to work until she got pregnant with her second baby. "It was really meaningful for me to be allowed to work with my child," she said. However, with one baby in tow and a second pregnancy, the work became too hard, and Brooke became too exhausted to keep doing it.

When we first spoke, Brooke's second child was only a few months old. She told me she had to adjust her expectations significantly for what she would be able to do while tending to her baby and growing toddler. She didn't plan to work on the farm with them at first but hoped to incorporate them into her work in her personal garden. "The stakes are a bit lower if it's just my own garden versus on the farm, where I need to transplant a certain number of flats and now I have

With a baby and a toddler, Brooke can spend a few hours a week packing CSA bags but is realistic about how much more farm work she can take on.

my kids and—oops—I only got half a flat done," she said. "So I'm going to give it a try on our own little garden first, see what happens, and then maybe pick up some extra farming hours for the organization as I can with them."

Overall, for anyone anticipating working with a baby, Brooke suggested setting expectations very low and then hoping you can do more than you anticipated. "My husband and I thought we would be able to work more with our child than what ended up being possible," she said. "So plan on having more coverage than you think you need. And then if you don't need it, great, but if you do need it, you have it."

DISCUSSION AND JOURNALING QUESTIONS

▶ *If you are anticipating having a baby, what are your current expectations for early parenthood? Did anything in this chapter surprise or concern you? Have you spent much time around babies or young children?*

▶ *What are your plans for addressing a baby's needs on your farm while still balancing the work that needs to be done? If you have a co-parent, how can the two of you delegate and share the work of parenting and farming/homesteading? What is your plan for taking care of yourselves, too, in terms of sleep, food, personal time, and so on?*

▶ *If you are parenting a baby, or have done so before, what have been your experiences? What might you share with someone else about the process or do differently another time?*

CHAPTER

10

ARRANGING
CHILDCARE

CHILDCARE IS REAL WORK, especially in the early years. Taking care of babies and children requires an understanding of their needs and the ability to be present to meet those needs so that they can be safe, healthy, and happy.

When farmers decide to have children, one of their biggest new and ongoing questions is: "Who watches the children?" The answer will evolve over time as kids and families grow, but until sometime in the early teen years, it will be necessary to answer this question for every moment of every day.

Solutions vary widely, and I'll present them in this chapter with voices from farmers sharing what's worked well or been hard about each of them. The reality is that most families use a mix of options—perhaps some extended family help one day and then paid help from a nanny another day. I'm presenting the basic options starting closest to home (parents doing care) and then working outward from there, but that order isn't intended to prioritize any of these solutions over another. The best solution is always the one that *works* for a particular family.

COMBINING FARM WORK WITH CHILDCARE

Although our society seems to think that farming and parenting can be done at the same time, many farmers find it very hard to work while providing childcare—especially for babies and toddlers, who have almost constant needs. Not only is working while watching children stressful and difficult, but it is also less safe for everyone. According to the National Children's Center for Rural and Agricultural Health and Safety, the safest place for a child is *away* from farm workspaces. This is especially true on larger, commercially oriented farms where there is machinery and lots of activity.

Small-scale farmers and homesteaders, however, do sometimes combine work and parenting, especially in contexts when it is okay for work to be done slowly or with constant interruptions. For some parents, integrating children into their tasks has always been one of the goals, and they've learned how to navigate their workload in a way that prioritizes safety for their children. To do so, they often sacrifice goals of speed, productivity, and efficiency.

Sarah Kostyu's 10 children range in age from 3 months to 19 years. She and her husband, Bret, operate K7 Farm, a 15-acre farm where they grow almost all their own food. Sarah also sells some products off the farm, provides processing services to deer hunters, and offers classes in homesteading. Bret is a truck driver and gone most of the week, meaning that she balances managing their farm with watching her children.

"Farming and 'mom-ing' can be difficult," Sarah said. "But there are a few things I've learned over the years—it may not all get done today, but there is always tomorrow." She wears her babies in a sling when it is safe to do so or makes strategic use of strollers and portable cribs to keep her babies nearby while she works in the garden. She stays attentive to their needs, making sure everyone is in the shade and has protection from insects. As they get older, she provides safe play opportunities. "I created a 'tot lot' in my garden one year,

WORKING WITH KIDS

Young children often enjoy being with parents for safe tasks, but adults must consider kids' needs while working.

WHEN YOU MUST HAVE CHILDCARE

While some parents can find a balance between watching their children and doing certain kinds of farm work, there are times when it's safest (for everyone) to give your full attention to farming and find another person to oversee your child, whether that's another parent or a babysitter. Use childcare for any task that carries potential physical risk. Some examples:

Doing any kind of tractor or machinery work

Vehicles, such as tractors and ATVs, are the primary cause of injury to children on farms. Vehicles present many potential hazards to children, including the risk of being run over, falling off moving equipment, and being injured from noise and vibration. Machinery and older tractors that are sometimes kept in use on small farms can pose extra risks because they usually have many fewer "safety" features like guards and kill switches. Keep children far away when you're operating machinery. Do not give children rides on machinery.

Working with large or potentially aggressive animals

This includes obviously dangerous animals such as bulls and rams, but even calmer large animals such as cows and goats can be a hazard to small people if they get underfoot. Animals are the second biggest cause of injury to children on farms.

Applying fertilizers or pesticides to crops

Stay current on your applicator's license if you need one to use your inputs. Make sure you know exactly what you're applying to your crops, and always read the Safety Data Sheet (SDS). Keep children away during the application process and out of any treated crops.

"I was surprised at how impossible it was to farm and watch our kids. It's easy to feel guilty that we should be able to do both, because it seems like some people do it. But I don't know, maybe they actually don't. Or maybe it's just different kids and different operations."

—AMY FRYE

complete with playhouses, tilled ground for cars to drive on and kids to dig in, and a kiddie pool and play set," she told me.

Parents can sometimes make use of naps and hours after bedtime to get work done without relying on others for childcare. John McCafferty of Pleasant River Produce in New Zealand often harvested while his young daughter slept nearby in the house. He brought a baby monitor with him in case she woke and needed him. He'd even work wearing a headlamp after dark. "There was something I really loved about it. During the day you can see everything, so you can be distracted by all the different things you have to do," John said. "Whereas when you've got a head torch and you're just picking some kale, it's almost meditative."

While he worked during naps and with his daughter around, John also had help from family and eventually sent his daughter to childcare as well. Again, most farmer-parents use multiple childcare options, working *with* children generally just a minority of the time.

> *"We have the exact same number of work hours a week and the same number of parenting hours a week and then hopefully some time together as a family, too."*
>
> **—HANAKO MYERS**

Many people reported that farming with children in tow was not an option at all, even for folks who thought it might be doable before becoming parents.

TAKE TURNS WORKING AND PARENTING

When two parents are involved in the farming, one option is to take turns working and caring for the children. Casey and I chose this option when we had our son, at least at first, in part because of our finances but also because we both wanted to be the first caregivers for our child—we wanted that time with him, and we had the flexibility in our operations to make that possible.

In our case, I stepped back from more of the physical farm work, but I continued to manage all the administrative and marketing work I'd always done. I found that even computer work and paying bills was difficult to do with a baby nearby, so in the first years we took turns doing childcare or working. Overall, Casey worked more and I hung out with the baby more, but several times a week, Casey took Rusty so that I could focus on work. In those times, Casey often carried Rusty in a sling and did light farm tasks that were less essential and could be interrupted.

Hanako Myers and Marko Colby split parenting duties equally in the first year after adopting their son. Without knowing exactly when they'd become parents, they weren't able to plan for parental leave even though they wanted to spend as much time as possible with their new baby. When he finally arrived in June 2020, COVID-19 pandemic restrictions and precautions took even part-time childcare off the table. "Obviously we immediately had to work way less than we normally did," Hanako said, but they did both still work, taking turns. After the first year, they started hiring childcare for a few days a week, but they continued to share the balance of parenting and working outside those hours.

MANAGING ON-FARM CHILDCARE

Some farmers hire nannies or have extended family who can come and help them on the farm. Many farmers said this was a great option when their children were babies because it allowed them to be nearby to nurse or be available as needed.

Hanako and Marko now have childcare for their son six partial days a week, right on the farm, and she loves that they are still able to see him throughout the day. "When he is with his childcare provider, we see him zooming by on his bike. He says hi and blows kisses," she said.

"We needed childcare and I wasn't finding anyone, and my husband said, 'We're not using our best tool, which is your Instagram account.' So I posted our baby's photo once even though we don't post about him; and we got a nanny out of it."

—TARA CHAPMAN

Casey and I started hiring a part-time babysitter once Rusty turned one. In some years, it was a person who came one afternoon a week so that I could focus on my administrative work without taking Casey out of the fields, but eventually we had a person coming two days a week to watch both our children so that I could get bigger projects done and work in the fields again.

Jordan Goldsmith of Moonrose Farm said that her mom comes to the farm to help with her daughter. "My mom comes three days a week, but only half days—just in the afternoon so that my wife and I can have a little bit of reprieve," she said. "Other than that, we're just switching off based on what needs to get done with childcare at this time."

Jordan said there are advantages and disadvantages to childcare happening near her workspace. "Her help has been good, but it's not as separate as daycare. She still comes out to see us with the baby and asks questions because it's been a long time since she's had kids," she said. "So it wasn't just, 'Here, take my kid so I can work.' I still stopped and nursed every two hours in the field. She brought me the baby and I hopped off the tractor and nursed and then handed her back. So I didn't really get to pay full attention to what I was doing for long stretches."

Tara Chapman of Two Hives Honey also hired an on-farm nanny after realizing that her ability to work was very limited with a baby. "I hired her for 20 hours a week and I thought, 'We probably only need 15, but we'll start with 20 and see how it goes,'" she remembered. "And then by the end of the week, I was like, 'I need her more.' And I just kept inching up her hours week by week until she was full-time."

Tara eventually switched to off-farm care because having her son at the farm was complicated during the workday. "We did in-home care until he was 14 or 15 months old, and then it got difficult because I'm always around, and he knew that and was clingy," she said. "I was hiding from him because he always wanted to be with me."

> *"It's been tricky to find childcare that aligns with our values. We did find a daycare/preschool for our sons that we like, but it's a 25-minute drive away from the farm, so we share driving duties."*
>
> —CHRISTINA MENCHINI

ARRANGING OFF-FARM CHILDCARE

Off-farm childcare, whether at a daycare or a family member's house, is an option many farmers choose. Elise Bortz of Elysian Fields Farm encouraged her mother to move nearby even before she had children. When her first child was born, Elise took parental leave and then briefly hired a nanny until her mother retired and was able to provide full-time care at her home for Elise's child. Elise said that having her child not with her on-site was important for her ability to manage her farm.

"When I'm here, I'm moving a million miles an hour," Elise said. "I'm the manager and I've got employees, but I'm right there with them. I'm doing everything they're doing. Or there are things that only I do. I'm the only one who drives the tractor and does all the bed prep. So it just felt like my attention would be divided—I wouldn't be good or effective at either job if I was trying to do them both at the same time."

Elise had her mom living nearby, which was fortunate, as she said that childcare can be hard to find in her area. She recommends parents (or prospective parents) research options well before they need it. "Some folks don't do that and then it's like, 'Oh no, this is expensive!'" she said. "Or they find they had to sign up for childcare two years in advance and be on the wait list. Things just fill up so quickly around here."

According to researchers Shoshanah Inwood and Florence Becot, two-thirds of farming families report having had challenges finding childcare. In their 2023 survey of 860 farm and ranch families, 77 percent of farmers reported that lack of childcare affects ability to get farm work done. "Most farms are located in rural communities, so they tend to have fewer childcare options," said Shoshanah. "And when options do exist, oftentimes they're structured for a typical nine-to-five workweek, Monday through Friday. And we know that farming often occurs after those times or on the weekends."

And, of course, when looking for childcare, farmers want to feel comfortable with the people and setting where they will be leaving their children.

CHILDCARE IS EXPENSIVE

One way or another, taking care of kids costs money. If one parent steps back from work, it may require the hiring of one or more employees to cover the gap. If parents decide to hire childcare, then that will cost money—and for many it is more money than they might expect.

Amy Frye said she had help from family for her kids' care and yet she still found herself piecing together extra paid childcare and preschool to provide enough coverage. "If you had told me when I was young how much I would spend on childcare, I would have said there's no possible way," she said.

Tory Shelley found an affordable home-based daycare she likes, but it is not open on Saturdays, a day when she works managing Featherbed Lane Farm's CSA pickup. So she has to hire a nanny one day a week as well, which costs much more. "I make four dollars an hour after paying the nanny, and she's giving me a deal." She said the cost of childcare is part of why she has continued to work only four days a week as a single mom. Tory hopes that when her daughter is old enough to go to school, she'll be able to work full-time again.

For some farmers, the high cost and low availability of childcare limit how flexible they can be with their decisions. Corinne Hansch and her husband took the shared parenting/working approach at Lovin' Mama Farm in part because of those challenges. She said she brought up questions about working with kids at a farming event when her children were young. "I suggested the topic of talking about people farming with kids, and people straight up laughed at me and said, 'How about a babysitter?' And I thought, 'Well, we're on food stamps. We cannot afford a babysitter.' Farmers deserve the chance to have a family."

In some parts of the world, farmers can make use of free or subsidized childcare. John McCafferty was a single father raising his daughter in New Zealand, where children receive 20 hours per week of free childcare from age three through the start of full-time schooling. Emily Board and Dan Brisebois are raising their three children on Tourne-Sol Cooperative Farm in Quebec, where subsidized childcare is available on a sliding scale. All the parents who are co-owners have been able to send their children to the same nearby daycare center, which is quite affordable.

> **The BEST thing about family farming is...**
>
> *Having the kids grow up in an edible wonderland.*
>
> JOHN McCAFFERTY,
> PLEASANT RIVER PRODUCE

NEEDS CHANGE AS KIDS GROW

However, even in situations where family can help or childcare is subsidized, every year brings new needs and new situations to sort out. For example, while Emily Board and Dan Brisebois have a great childcare solution for their young children, once the kids start school, they have to plan for their summer breaks—and, of course, summers are the busiest season for their work. They piece childcare together with day camps and visits to grandparents, but it has meant that Dan works less in summer simply because he is driving kids around and picking them up. "There's no fantastic solution for summer work hours with the kids," Emily said. They live near their farm and wonder whether summers with their older kids might be easier if they actually lived *on* the property. "But the way our farm is set up, we don't have a bunch of extra space," Emily said. "People are working everywhere."

As discussed in Chapter 2, as children grow older and more responsible, their need for direct supervision begins to change. More work time is possible while kids play safely nearby. When our children both reached elementary-school age, Casey and I started using two-way radios with them so they could be at the house or in the yard while we worked in our field. In our case, our field is immediately in front of our house, so we were physically still quite close, but the radios allowed us

"We eat breakfast, lunch, and dinner together every day, which is so special."

—HANAKO MYERS

all to check in with each other regularly without needing to run back and forth.

As our children became more independent and easier to supervise, they started spending more time with my parents, who live next door. Their help allowed Casey and me to do our CSA distribution with both of us present and focused.

At some point, older children can also help watch younger children. And as children become tweens and teens, they are usually mature enough to be quite independent, giving farmer-parents more time to work without needing to be as conscious of watching children or arranging childcare.

The years when children's needs are most demanding pass quickly, but they can be intense periods for parents and for a farm. Planning ahead, being flexible, and having as many options as possible can help parents navigate those challenges.

DISCUSSION AND JOURNALING QUESTIONS

▶ *What are all your childcare options now? How do you feel about them? What are the pros and cons of each one? What are the barriers to getting the childcare hours you need?*

▶ *Do you anticipate working with your child nearby? How will you set yourself up for flexibility and realistic expectations for productivity in that time?*

▶ *If you already have children, what strategies have you used for working with them nearby or for childcare? What has worked or not worked? How did those strategies change as your children grew?*

Hanako Myers
Midori Farm
Quilcene, Washington

NAVIGATING WORK AND FAMILY DYNAMICS

AS SHOULD BE CLEAR by this point in this book, having children changed everything for Casey and me, as it does for most people. Not only did we have to grow into new people with a completely new set of responsibilities and lifestyle, but we also had to continually adjust our farm to accommodate those changes.

There are many reasons having children might inspire farmers to change how they operate their farm businesses, many of which relate to previous chapters in this book. They might want to achieve more balance in their lives to have more time to spend with the children (see Chapter 6) or they might need to adjust their operations to solve childcare needs (see Chapter 10). Some changes might be more related to relationships with employees or customers and how intimately farmers want to share their new family lives with others.

Circumstances vary widely between individual farms, but in this chapter, I want to share some specific examples of the ways farmers planned and operated their farms after becoming parents.

Over time, Benina Montes's role became focused on special projects that allow her to continue thinking about the big-picture future of the farm while giving her the flexibility to tend to the needs of her four children.

NEW RESPONSIBILITIES, CHANGING ROLES

When we had our first child, my role on the farm changed in big ways. I'd always overseen all our administrative tasks: managing organic certification, bookkeeping, CSA customer communication, advertising, web management, and so on. But those were tasks that I could fit into evening hours or one day a week. I spent my days side by side with Casey in the fields and at market.

After we became parents, it felt like it made sense to shift my field duties to an employee so that I could be the primary caregiver for our baby. Casey did enough baby care that I could continue to do the business management. While I eventually did get back into the fields part-time, I always remained the "default" parent—the one who stayed with the kids when they were sick or if our babysitter had to cancel. I also took the lead on homeschooling our children, which required me to dedicate time to doing lessons with them during the school year.

Our balance was the right choice for our farm and family, but it represented a big shift in my identity and, for me and Casey, a big shift in our working relationship. Finding time to meet and talk about the farm got increasingly difficult, and so we more often just trusted each other to make good decisions in our separate spheres of the farm.

Other farmers experienced a similar shift toward "inside" farm work when becoming a parent. Benina Montes of Burroughs Family Farms in California hired a farm manager after having children. "I had meetings," she said, "but I just talked to them and set goals and asked questions. They were doing a lot more of the day-to-day." Now that her children are all in school, she is moving back into more daily operations and tasks.

Katrina McQuail of Meeting Place Organic Farm in Ontario also shifted to a more managerial role after having children. "I'm the person who has the plan for the farm in my head," she said. "I have the high-level, big-picture stuff, but I'm not getting to execute a lot of the day-to-day." Even when she has childcare, Katrina ends up prioritizing the farm management, something she can't do with her children present. "It means that I'm still not the person out *doing*, because it's easier for me to hand off feeding livestock or repairing something than it is for me to transfer the management piece."

"I don't feel like I'm farming as much anymore, and that's hard."

—KATRINA McQUAIL

> *"People have a life outside of work and it's more important than what they do on my farm. That's a perspective I just didn't have before I had a child."*
>
> —TARA CHAPMAN

CHANGES IN EMPLOYEE RELATIONS

Becoming a parent can alter a farmer's relationship with their employees or coworkers. After the birth of our second child, Casey and I found that we needed more privacy for our family and made some big changes in how we interacted with our crew—including letting go two young people who did not respond well to the stress during the week of the birth. Our home is in the middle of our farm, which means our crew interacted constantly with our family life, and we wanted that to be positive for everyone. We also wanted to create a sense of a bubble around our house, so we asked our employees to come to the house or yard only when explicitly invited. Those small changes helped us have good relationships with our employees going forward.

Amy Frye of Boldly Grown Farm in Washington has also felt occasional distance with her employees since becoming a parent. "It's harder for me to feel like I connect with our young employees in their twenties who don't have kids," she said. "And it makes me feel old. It's hard for me to go out and harvest kale and talk with them about what they did at the bar."

She said she also feels like younger employees don't always understand why she can't be in the field as she balances managing the farm with making sure kids get to daycare or school. "It's hard to convey what a business owner does, even outside of kids and the childcare juggle and all that," she said. "I don't expect them to get it, but it's still hard to feel like there's a disconnect there. There's the boss guilt feeling of 'I wish I could be out harvesting kale with you more.' I hope that if they have kids in the future, they'll look back and finally realize, 'That was crazy what they were doing.'"

> **The BEST thing about family farming is...**
>
> *Having a great place to go with our kids and have them learn so much about plants, seeds, and nature.*
>
> DAN BRISEBOIS, TOURNE-SOL COOPERATIVE FARM

Having children can also give a farmer a new perspective about the importance of their employees' personal lives. Tara Chapman of Two Hives Honey in Texas said she has learned to offer her employees, especially those with children, more flexibility. She also started offering health insurance to her year-round employees.

Katrina McQuail values her employees' ability to get along with her family alongside their ability to farm. "It's okay that I'm not getting every penny of efficiency out of my staff," she said. "Their ability to be around the kids makes it easier for me to communicate with them."

She also appreciates her employees' ability to be independent workers because she needs tasks to be done even if she can't follow up the way she used to. "I need to have people to whom I can say, 'This needs to happen,'" she said. "'Here are the four points that you need to know about, and if these things get hit, you can decide how the rest of it gets done.'"

Hanako Myers of Midori Farm in Washington said that becoming a parent has been an opportunity for her to improve her organizational skills. She knows that some days family life will interrupt her ability to meet with her employees, and she plans so her staff

In addition to relying on her farm crew to help her stay organized, Hanako Myers also appreciates the ways her employees interact with her son on the farm. "I think people really love to see him growing."

will always know what to do. "Rather than just show the reality of my chaos, I try to have a system that's very organized," she said. "I think it creates a more enjoyable workplace and job for people."

EXPERIMENT WITH SCALE

Upon becoming parents, many farmers want more balance in their life than they needed before. One way to find that balance is to experiment with scale to find the "sweet spot" for their situation. In this regard, what works for one farm family will be different from what works for another. Much depends on the land base, marketing model, availability of reliable skilled employees, and other key factors.

Corinne Hansch of Lovin' Mama Farm in New York said experimenting with scale was an important part of freeing up more time for her and her husband to be with their three children. "As our business has scaled up, our work/life balance has gotten better," she said. Finding that balance feels even more urgent to Corinne now that her oldest is 16. "It's kind of scary, because he's almost grown up, and I've been farming his whole childhood." But with a larger scale that can support more employees, she and her husband have gained more flexibility to spend time with their kids beyond the context of farm work.

On our farm, Casey and I had the opposite experience. We expanded our operation almost every year until we were at our peak: managing 100 acres of mixed vegetables, orchards, pastures, and field crops with many employees on our payroll. This was the time when our life was very out of balance. While we had lots of people around to help, we still found that the scale and complexity of our diverse operation required us to be conscious of farm activities almost every waking moment of the day—and with a baby and toddler in the house, we felt stretched extremely thin.

After two years of operating at that scale, we simplified our operation significantly, reorganized our marketing, cut our acreage in half, and went to having just one employee. Those changes made a profound difference in our work and stress load, and our farm's profits actually went up.

John McCafferty of Pleasant River Produce in New Zealand also found himself preferring a smaller scale than he initially thought was necessary for his farm's viability. "There was one point where I always thought I needed to get bigger to make it work better. But it worked much better when I actually started to just improve the space I was in and not try and keep on stretching out," he said. "And having a small farm footprint is quite handy, for my child can be anywhere within that space and I know they're safe."

Again, the goal is to experiment and find that sweet spot that, for whatever reason, works with your situation so that you can enjoy your farm *and* enjoy life with your family.

BE INTENTIONAL ABOUT THE INTERNET

It's very likely that you and/or your farm have an internet presence: a website, email newsletter, and/or social media accounts. For many farmers, these outlets are opportunities to share a more intimate view of their farm and their work with their customers and others.

When you add children to a farm, it may seem natural to include images and stories of the children in such content. There are many reasons to do this: In addition to being part of your life and stories, children become part of the farm and its stories. Plus, photos of babies and kids make people happy. For farm families where children are highly integrated into the farm activities, it can be joyful to include them.

There is no right or wrong choice when it comes to sharing images of children on the internet. However, I encourage you to think carefully about how and when you share. Consider the unique dynamics of your situation.

- What are your farm's online platforms, and who sees them?

- What kind of pictures of your family and your farm do you want to share?

- How much do you want people to know about your family?

- Are your children old enough that you can ask them about their preference?

- Do you want to set boundaries in terms of what family information is shared online, and who (family members, childcare providers, employees) do you need to communicate with about that?

In our case, it felt best to keep our children a side story in the information we shared about our farm. I kept a regular blog for our farm, and I posted occasionally about the children there, too, but the farm remained the focus. I also limited *where* I shared. Most of our farm business came from word of mouth, so I didn't do much promotion of our farm on social media.

(Although it wasn't a concern of mine at the time, some people avoid posting images of children on social media because of uncertainties around who owns those images and how they might be used.)

We also asked our employees not to post about our family or the farm on their social media accounts without our permission. Since our farm was also our home, we wanted to have a sense of privacy here.

Katrina McQuail and her husband decided from the beginning that they wouldn't share photos of their young children on the internet. "At some point, they can make an educated, conscious decision about how they want to be on the internet, but until then, what purpose does it serve?"

They do include family photos sometimes in their Meeting Place Organic Farm emails and share tidbits about their family when writing about the farm. "I try to find the balance of being real and authentic without oversharing or sharing stuff that might create an issue for our kids down the road," Katrina said. "It's a balance, because my journey as a parent is mine. But my farm business doesn't need me to share all of that with our customers."

Tara Chapman and her husband also decided not to share about their baby on the internet or on Two Hives's social media accounts. She said this has significantly changed how she posts on Instagram, which used to be a very intimate outlet for her. "How do I talk about my life and what I'm doing and what's happening when everything is so intertwined with this little guy? But I don't think it's fair for me to share his stories and his photo and his journey for thousands of people to see." She told me she's still navigating this new path.

There are other considerations about the consequences of sharing images of our families. Christina Menchini of Campfire Farms does share photos of her children but tries to make sure she's depicting their farm and life accurately. "I don't want to make it seem like we are farming with our children in the field. I consumed too many of those images, and that way of farming with kids didn't work out for me," she said. "I'll use them a little bit, but I don't want to paint a picture that's not true."

> "Having a store on the farm is completely related to having kids. I want it near our house so I can hear someone come up the lane and then go meet them in the store."
>
> —KATRINA McQUAIL

MAKE DECISIONS THAT WORK FOR YOU

Rather than dramatically scaling up or down, sometimes simply streamlining operations can help increase profits and provide more time. This can be especially true on a farm that starts with multiple moving parts and has had time to see which ones have proven the most successful.

Emily Board and Dan Brisebois are two of the 10 owners of Tourne-Sol Cooperative Farm in Quebec. All the co-owners are now parents, and they decided to quit selling at farmers' markets and focus on their farm's CSA program and seed company. "One of the reasons was that it was challenging to staff markets," said Emily. But she said it was also about accommodating family life. "We have young kids and want to do family things on the weekends."

They also started taking Fridays as half days for the whole farm, a move that began because of temporary overstaffing and then continued due to worry about burnout during the stressful times of the COVID-19 pandemic. "People love finishing at noon," Dan said. "They can go to the bank or do other errands. Or they can have a long weekend. We've built our farm around planning and management so that we don't burn ourselves out. We can have lives." Having plenty of owners and staff has also helped them make these kinds of choices.

Katrina McQuail has changed how her farm distributes meat in order to provide her more time on the farm. She and her parents used to personally drive meat orders to their customers' homes, but with three children, she can no longer justify using her valuable time driving. "We've started using a delivery service," she said. "I miss seeing our customers—the in-person relationship—but it's meant that I can ship meat more frequently." She now sends orders weekly and is planning an on-farm store and more events to bring work closer to home and build community for her family.

Many of the decisions parent-farmers make to streamline their operations end up being profitable and positive on many levels, but the decisions are ultimately driven by the desire to provide more time to be with their children.

DISCUSSION AND JOURNALING QUESTIONS

▶ *If you are already a parent, how has your role on your farm changed since having children? Are there parts of your former role that you want to get back to someday?*

▶ *If you have employees or coworkers who work around your children, what are your expectations or hopes for the way they interact with your family? How can you communicate about your expectations in this regard?*

▶ *Are there any places in your farm's operation where you can streamline? Or would hiring more employees or scaling up or down provide you more flexibility and time?*

Daisy Remington
Auckland, New Zealand

STARTING A
FARM
AFTER HAVING
KIDS

SO FAR, I'VE SHARED PERSPECTIVES on raising children after establishing a farm. But many farm families have children before starting their farms, too. For some people, starting a farm is a longtime career goal that was realized after they started a family simply because of life circumstances and timing. For others, the path to farming becomes clear as family needs arise.

Daisy Remington's farming journey began when her older child wasn't thriving in his first year of school in suburban New Zealand. When she and her husband, Russell Clarke, learned that their son was on the autism spectrum, Daisy decided to homeschool him in ways better suited to his needs. She found that immersion in nature and concrete hands-on learning were positive for him and his younger sister. Daisy also wanted to feed her family good-quality food—she grew as much as she could in her small yard but still had to purchase most of it.

"Trying to eat healthfully in New Zealand is not cheap. I'm growing this little bit of food," Daisy remembered, "and I am taking these kids to reserves [parks] all the time." She decided that moving to a farm was the answer to their lifestyle goals.

Sarah Kostyu of K7 Farm in Michigan had a similar trajectory that began the night her first child was born. "As a first-time nursing mother, I wanted to be sure the foods I ate were healthy to nourish me, so I could nourish her," she said. "I made my very first from-scratch meal that night and haven't looked back!" Sarah's interest in eating well led to a desire to grow her family's food. "We eventually outgrew our backyard's capacity to grow food and decided we should buy a farm because clearly this was a lifestyle that was proving to be no passing fancy!"

LOOKING FOR THE RIGHT PLACE

Finding a place to farm can be a very challenging first step. Some regions have more farmable land than others, and prices to buy or rent can vary widely. And when a family decides to farm, their children also become a consideration in searching for the right location.

Land is one of the biggest factors in determining what your farming experience will be like. Will you live on your land or at another site nearby? What kind of home will your family have when you first move here (house? yurt? nothing?)? How much infrastructure will you have to develop? How much will you need to improve the soil? How far will you need to travel to markets? And, of course, for the children, what kind of landscape will shape their childhood?

Daisy and her family spent two years searching for the right property for their farm home. They were looking for a place where they could raise both livestock and crops, but Daisy also wanted a farm that was more or less ready in terms of housing and infrastructure. Her husband, Russell, would continue to work off the farm, so they needed a place that was safe for her to farm with two young children around. "I didn't want to have to be building shelters and putting up fencing while also doing school and having kids around."

> *"We needed the basics to be in place when we moved to our farm. I needed to know where our water was coming from. I needed to know where the animals were going to go."*

—DAISY REMINGTON

Other considerations come into play for families, too, especially budget limitations, which might lead some to prioritize differently. Bil Thorn and Kate Harwell had two toddlers when they decided to buy 120 acres in northern California and start a rustic homestead. The land was very remote—25 miles down a dirt road and across two rivers that they had to drive through. Two years later, they moved to a property slightly closer to the main road for easier access to town, but both properties were unimproved land where they lived in tents and later a modified greenhouse. At the second property, the homestead site was up a hill too steep to drive, requiring them to pack in all their supplies. "We were desperate not to be renting and to have something of our own," Kate said. "We were willing to go to those lengths. If we have to walk to our property, we will."

On their land, Kate and Bil cultivated a 200- by 70-foot garden plot, planted fruit trees, and kept chickens, goats, and sheep. The children were homeschooled with support through the local school and helped on the property. But eventually California's drought caused their water source to run dry, and the family started looking for new land with plenty of water. Again, their budget steered them, and they found their current farm, Sky Island Farm, in Washington. This land also had a house and barn and was closer to town, giving them more options for commercial growing and marketing in Seattle.

"We live the way we do for our kids, so that we can be home with them, but also so that they can have a business to run later, if they want. And living a more natural way of life is better for children."

—BIL THORN AND KATE HARWELL

CONSIDERING COMMUNITY

In addition to considering the aspects of the land and infrastructure, many parents also factor in the wider environment and community of their potential farm locations, with kids and family life in mind.

Alyson Larkin and her family used to rent a house in a suburb outside Portland, Oregon, where they had room for a large garden. When their landlords didn't renew their lease because they wanted to live in the house themselves, the family had to move, and Alyson decided they should look for a place with even more space to grow. "I knew deep down that I wanted to be on land and raise my children where they had the freedom to just be kids and have green space," she said.

She started researching the nearby agricultural communities that were closer to her work as a doula at a rural birth center. She wanted to make sure the culture of their future community would be a positive one for their family. One of the towns they explored didn't feel like a good fit, but another one did. "McMinnville felt family oriented," Alyson said. "It felt like there was more going on for families through the parks and recreation department. We heard good things about the school district."

Alyson and her husband, Andrew, responded to a Craigslist ad for a house to rent on Wingspan Farm, a large property just outside McMinnville shared by two other households. The farm has pasture and growing spaces on the lower ground and a large, forested area on a hillside. Alyson knew it was the right choice before even getting out of the car on their first visit. "I was at the peak of the driveway to the farm and I was like, 'I'm already a yes, I don't have to see the house or the inside of the house,'" Alyson said. "It has a big place to garden, the forest, fields to run in. There's a creek, a pond—it was like heaven handed to us."

The adjustment to living in a more rural place was daunting at first in terms of making new relationships. "But I quickly found a great community here," Alyson said. "And it helped that we were moving to a huge piece of land with community already built into it." There were other kids the same ages as hers on the land, and they became friends easily.

Alyson is grateful for the community support with the farming activities. Everyone on the land helps care for the animals and the two-acre garden together. "Gardening was the biggest piece of being in community," she said. "I don't think I could grow a garden at that scale, just me and my husband." The families sharing the property also help carpool kids to school in town and for other activities.

"It's wonderful to be in community on a farm and share the responsibility, the fun, and the joy."

—ALYSON LARKIN

(5) TIPS TO HELP KIDS ADJUST

1 Do some practice farming.

If you already have children and want to start a farm or move to land in the future, consider how you can start incorporating that kind of work or play into your life now to help prepare them. Possibilities: Plant vegetables in window boxes, read picture books about farming and seasonal living (see pages 57–59 for suggestions), buy a CSA share from a local farm, volunteer at a farm, or rent a plot in a community garden. Alyson Larkin and her family gardened on a large scale at a nearby community plot before they moved to Wingspan Farm, so her young children already understood some of the rhythms of workdays and growing.

2 Visit your future farm before moving.

Once you've found a place to farm or homestead, visit the location as many times as possible before moving there. "We were out here several times before we moved out," Alyson said about the transition to the farm, where they rent one of three houses on the land. "We toured the farm and had several dinners out here so that the kids got to know everybody." They also visited the nearby city, McMinnville, and checked out the schools.

3 Empathize with the transition.

Most farmers report that their children are delighted to move to a farm and have more space to roam and play. But the transition to a new place and lifestyle can be rough for some children (and for some adults, too!). If that's the case, make space for their transition feelings, even the hard ones. Daisy Remington's daughter was four when they moved from a suburban life to their

New Zealand farm. At first, she was sad, missing what was familiar and feeling overwhelmed by learning so many new things. "We talked about it a lot," Daisy said. "We talked about the things she missed. I never told her to buck up or reminded her this place is so great. I just acknowledged that she was sad."

4 Bring familiar elements to the new place.

Daisy said she also offered to help her daughter bring familiar things into their new life on the farm. "What are some of the things we can bring here to help this feel more like home?" Daisy asked her. These familiar elements might be physical objects that come with your family to the new home: furniture, favorite books, a special blanket. But you can also invite old friends or family to visit to help children remember that elements of their lives remain stable even with the change in location.

5 Give kids time to transition.

Everyone—children and adults alike—needs time to grow into a new home and lifestyle. But seeing the joys of each season return in a new year can help grow new attachments and familiarity. Daisy said that during her family's second summer on their farm, things shifted for her daughter. "She was going out and getting blackberries and coming back with scratches on her hand and blue all over her face," Daisy said. "And she said, 'Actually, I think it's okay.'"

WHAT AGE IS BEST?

Making the move to a farm can feel daunting when kids are very young and needing lots of attention and care. However, the three families I've mentioned so far had young children when they did so and reported relatively easy transitions to farm life. Young children are naturally curious, and having the expanded outdoor play area and interesting things to see and do is usually (or eventually) a welcome lifestyle change.

But Kate Harwell and Bil Thorn have known families that had a harder time making the transition, especially with older children. "I have seen some people bring older children into a homestead situation and the kids hated it," Kate said, "because they've moved them away from town and their friends." Bil said the expectation that kids will do more active chores and work on a farm than in town can also be a shock, especially for kids who haven't done much physical work before. "The workload is so much heavier," he said. "I think that you have to start them young. Otherwise, you're going to deal with a mutiny."

Kate said it's important to be respectful of kids' experience: "If you have older kids, keep in mind their feelings and remember that forcing them into the farm lifestyle may not work out." She also suggested that finding land closer to town might be a higher priority so that kids can continue to maintain their social life and participate in activities.

Obviously, older kids *can* adjust to farm life, and many flourish. School groups often come out to Sky Island Farm, and Kate noted there are always several in the group who seem to love the farm experience more than others: "They say, 'Wow, this lifestyle's really cool. I could do this.'" Some of them have come back to intern on the farm.

Older kids and teens can be highly capable, which can make the transition to a farm easier for everyone involved if they are willing and able to chip in with chores right away. In this case, having older kids can certainly be a very positive factor in making a lifestyle shift as a family.

DISCUSSION AND JOURNALING QUESTIONS

▶ *If you don't yet have space for farming or homesteading with your family, take a moment and envision your dream space. What kinds of features or qualities does it have for you? What kinds of features or qualities does it have for your children?*

▶ *Now, looking at your answers to the questions above, what are your absolute must-haves? What might you be willing to let go?*

▶ *What kind of farming or growing work can you begin doing now to help transition your family and kids to a future experience?*

▶ *If your children are old enough, ask them to consider and share their thoughts and feelings about a potential shift in lifestyle.*

THE NEEDS OF
TWEENS
AND
TEENS

TWELVE-YEAR-OLD RUSTY ran inside one day last summer and announced that our raspberries were ripe and abundant. "We need to freeze some for winter!" he declared, and I agreed and then returned to whatever other pressing task needed my attention at that moment. Seeing that I wasn't making any immediate move to harvest the raspberries, later that afternoon Rusty gathered up containers from the kitchen and asked Dottie to join him in picking enough to freeze. After filling their containers, they carefully loaded their harvest into freezer bags without crushing any berries and laid them flat to freeze in a single layer.

Might I have gotten around to picking and freezing raspberries later? Yes, probably. But Rusty recognized a seasonal task and took initiative to complete it (and to organize help!), ensuring that the raspberries were put up in a timely manner—and we gratefully enjoyed them all winter long.

Rusty's ability to do work on his own is a hallmark of the farm tween/teen—a maturing child who has been raised immersed in the joy of seasonal eating and the work that makes it possible. He had waited and watched for ripening berries every summer of his life and helped us pick for our customers and for our household many times before, so by this time he knew exactly what needed to be done and when. Obviously, situations vary, but most of the farmers I've spoken with have found the tween/teen years of parenting to be incredibly gratifying because of scenarios like this. The hard work of balancing farming and parenting begins to feel like it produces "fruit" (in our case, literal fruit in our freezer).

But adolescence can bring new needs and challenges. Farm families address those in different ways, often finding that the farm itself provides many opportunities for young people to gain essential confidence and skills—while recognizing that tweens/teens might need more life off the farm, too.

KIDS CAN CONTRIBUTE

By ages 11 through 13, most children are growing new independence and competence, with increased levels of comprehension of complex tasks, improved motor skills, and longer attention spans for work. These are the ages when farmers report a profound shift in their kids' ability to help, making a big difference to the farm and family. While young children decidedly increase the workload, tweens can change the equation significantly—and that shift can just continue for many families through the teen years as children continue to grow, become stronger, and develop their own internal motivations to work.

Lyn Jacobs and her husband, Juvencio Argueta, raised their three children at their Oregon farm, La Finquita del Buho. The children are all young adults now (I interviewed two of them for Chapter 14), but Lyn remembers well the early days of expecting the kids to help with their farm's weekly CSA harvest. Her oldest, Jacob, was very helpful by 14, but when she tried to get her second child, Diego, to help at

age 11, he was still growing into the work. "He was just throwing things at his brother," she said. "We had to separate them." Lyn told Diego that she would start paying him once he could work well for two hours at a time. "Eventually he became one of my best workers."

Corinne Hansch observed the same shift in her children. She and her husband are raising three kids at Lovin' Mama Farm in New York. "Once children are 14 or 15, they're really young adults," she said. "They're contributing a lot."

Bil Thorn and Kate Harwell operate Sky Island Farm, in Washington, with plenty of help from their 16- and 18-year-old children, who have learned almost every task on the farm. They work full-time in summers. "Their level of involvement is completely integral to our operation," said Bil. When Bil and Kate hired employees to help grow their CSA operation, they soon realized that their own children were much more capable than anyone they were able to hire.

Corinne had a similar observation: "I'm pretty blown away by my kids' abilities as workers, but also just their common sense and life skills. They know how to use a broom. I've had employees show up and literally not know how to sweep a floor."

5 BIG IDEAS
FOR MEETING TEENS' NEEDS

1 Give them space to "play" in new ways.

Teens still like to play, but that play might look different: bigger, messier, louder. A farm property can be an amazing place to let a young person explore big projects and interests. Sometimes those projects can be farm related, but you can also give them space to pursue nonfarming interests, too. For example, when he was 13, our son, Rusty, started building bike trails with jumps around the edges of our fields. Other ideas: Set aside space for a soccer field, invite your child's band to practice in an outbuilding, or commission your child to paint a mural on the side of your barn.

2 Hire their friends.

Being with friends is a big priority for many tweens and teens. Corinne Hansch hired a few of her kids' friends to work at their farm part-time in summer. "They love it," she said. She does expect everyone to work hard. "But we also have fun, and they work only four hours a day." Teens might also enjoy working on crews and getting to know other employees, especially slightly older young adults who can be both friends and role models.

3 Include them in farm plans.

If your teens are working significant hours for the farm, ask them whether they want to have more input in seasonal farm planning as well. Bil Thorn and Kate Harwell include their 16- and 18-year-old in all their planning and have adjusted farm goals and enterprises based on their children's input. "We always take in the kids' considerations," said Kate. "We want this to be an enjoyable experience for them."

5 Check in with them daily.

As teens gain independence, be sure to keep checking in with them regularly just to chat and see how they are doing, perhaps during drives or while cleaning up after dinner together. Lyn Jacobs said she valued reading to her kids and tucking them into bed every night during their childhood, especially since her off-farm job and the farm work kept her busy all day. She continued some part of that rhythm even into their teen years, ensuring she had individual time with each of them.

"You think they don't need you, and they absolutely need you, but they won't ask," she said of her teens. She said sometimes challenges like depression are hard to spot when everyone's lives are busy with school, farming, and other work, and it's important to be present and provide opportunities for teens to open up. "Even if I just went into their room to say good night, it gave them that knowledge that I was there."

4 Admit when you need help.

At a certain point, some teens' physical abilities eclipse those of one or both of their parents—they might, for example, be taller or stronger. Having this recognized can be a confidence builder. "If I can't reach something or it's too heavy, my teens love to help," said Corinne. Similarly, your teens may develop interests and skills that you don't have, such as art and design or coding. Ask them (and even pay them) to help you design a new brochure for the farm or redesign the farm's website.

As discussed in Chapter 4, it's important to remember that children develop at their own pace. So even in these later years, it's essential to know your child well and adjust expectations appropriately based on their development and skills. This is especially important for any physically dangerous tasks. Some kids may surprise you with their maturity and ability, and others may require more patience.

As teens' skills grow, their work begins to fall into two categories: work that contributes to the family chores and work that offsets other paid labor on the farm and should be financially compensated—especially as a child's efforts become more professional.

TEENS BENEFIT FROM WORK

While new, more capable contributions are, of course, always welcome for a busy farm and household, there are also huge benefits for the tweens and teens themselves. One of the important developmental tasks of adolescence is working toward independence. In addition to continuing formal schooling, teens can fill these years with learning early work skills and beginning to make and save their own money. Being a part of a farm family can provide a way for young people to do both right at home.

Feeling like they are an important part of the farm can be a huge confidence builder. Lyn Jacobs said that her teens' friends sometimes came to the farm to help harvest, providing a unique opportunity for her children to demonstrate their knowledge: "They got to show their friends all the skills they had."

Working together on farm and garden projects can also provide an important bonding opportunity for parents and teenagers. As teens become more skilled, they can often put in longer work sessions alongside parents or other adults, providing opportunity for conversation to flow.

Alyson Larkin observed this about her 11- and 15-year-old sons: "As the kids have gotten older, their work time is longer and harder. When the teenagers are working with us in the garden or forest, we have great conversations." Working outside, Alyson said, allows them to have many kinds of interactions. "It's such a nice space to talk, whether we're being silly or having heavy conversations about what's happening in the world. It's good to do that out in the green space."

The physicality of work can be grounding for teens who have extra energy or need an outlet for stress. Corinne Hansch said one of her teenage sons likes to put on music and chop wood for a few hours. "He comes back and he's fulfilled," she said. "He did something, and we got him out of his room and out of the house."

EXPANDING LIFE BEYOND THE FARM

Of course, with the increased drive for independence that comes with adolescence, tweens and teens may desire more from life than playing and working on the farm with their family. This desire can mean a new set of burdens for parents or other caregivers who might now spend more time driving kids to and from activities. Depending on the family's proximity to town life, these drives can be a significant time commitment for everyone.

PROFILE:
WHEN THE FARMER IS A TEEN

What happens when the *farmer* is a teenager? That was the case for Sara Patterson, who started Red Acre Farm's CSA program when she was only 14. Her parents had moved from Los Angeles to an acre of land in rural Utah a few years earlier. "We moved here with zero intention to farm. I knew she'd have fun, and I wanted to read and detox from Los Angeles," said Symbria Patterson, Sara's mother.

But Sara was homeschooled and had lots of time to start growing plants, raising animals, and improving the land's dry soil. She had grown up visiting farmers' markets in California and remembered the vibrant local food scene there. Then, when a family friend started a CSA in Nevada, Sara fell in love with that marketing model. "We went down there, and I loved it. I was like, 'I want to do this,'" said Sara.

There weren't any farmers selling directly to consumers in their area in Utah at the time. "Local wasn't a thing here then," said Symbria. Sara agreed: "When we moved here, there really was only Walmart."

After experimenting with growing and selling produce, Sara started a CSA with four customer-members in 2009, a time when her parents were both busy with their own work. "I couldn't pay that much attention to her farming efforts at the time, but that whole summer, she was single-handedly putting these gorgeous baskets together," Symbria said.

"I just loved it," Sara said. Her growing and marketing methods have evolved a lot since she began, of course, as she's learned how to farm efficiently and professionally. "Now, when

I look back, I think, 'I would never do things like that. What was I thinking?' But when you're 14, really anything's possible. 'Dreams first, details later' has always been my motto."

Seeing Sara's success and dedication, Symbria decided to help Sara grow the CSA to 18 shares the next year. At the end of that second year, both parents saw the potential of what Sara had started.

"They came to me and said, 'If you think you can cover these expenses, we'll make this our work, too, and we'll all do this together,'" Sara said. "And so that's when they came in. It became our family's sole source of income." She was 16 at the time. That year she also bought the one-acre lot next door, doubling the farm's acreage.

Those early years were tight for the family as they built the farm, but Sara was able to travel to conferences and events in other states to meet other farmers and learn more. When she explained her unique situation, she would tell other farmers, "I'm a homeschooling project out of control."

Sara's father died when she was 20, at which point she realized she needed to really commit or change course because there were fewer other options for the family. "That's when I really had to make the decision," she said. "Because at this point, we still have to pay the bills and this is how we're paying them. So, is this how I'm going to do it, or am I going to do something else?"

Sara, now 28, is still a full-time farmer operating a full-diet style of CSA at Red Acre Farm. Since starting the farm, Sara has been able to meet many of her personal heroes, including farmer-authors Eliot Coleman and Kristin Kimball. In addition to gratitude for her parents' incredible trust and belief in her vision, she expressed gratitude for the work earlier generations of farmers did growing the local food movement and market farming.

"I wouldn't be where I am without all of those farmers who sacrificed so much for this movement," Sara said. "I'm just riding their coattails."

As teens mature, relationships with extended family members may evolve. My parents live next door and have always been involved in our kids' lives. However, as Rusty and Dottie grow into people capable of having conversations and developing their own interests, they spend even more time with their grandparents, working together on projects in Mimi and Pops's garden or shop.

Not every farm family can afford the time and money of a full life off the farm for every child, but every parent I spoke with respected these needs and did their best to support their teens' growth and interests. Corinne Hansch homeschools her children and sees the time they can spend off the farm with peers as important to their development as people: "I try to say yes as much as I can to social time."

Though Lyn Jacobs's kids helped with weekly harvests, she said they didn't all voluntarily help as much with other field tasks. Their reluctance to work was hard for her husband, Juvencio, who grew up in Honduras on a farm where he was expected to help. The couple worked to balance their expectations for their teens, navigating the kids' increased competence and responsibilities and their desire to have a full life. "You've got obligations and as a kid you should participate in the family endeavor," Lyn said. "But you should also be able to have fun and hang out with your friends." She observed that sometimes it seemed as though her kids spent more time at their friends' houses "because there was work here at home." Lyn said her kids were also involved with soccer, but their home is within a mile of their high school, making it easy for the family to support their athletic activities and attend games.

Another way for teens to expand their life beyond their immediate family unit is to grow relationships with adults other than their parents. This need can be met on the farm itself through positive relationships with farm employees, but adolescence is also a time when teens benefit from relationships with coaches, teachers, youth group leaders, and other adults not connected with the farm at all. Those relationships can help them see themselves in new ways.

All the parents I spoke with also emphasized the need for some level of privacy for older kids. They observed their teens wanting to spend more time alone, both to work on schoolwork and to have conversations with friends, have space to develop who they are, and process some of the big emotions that accompany puberty. Those who could do so found it valuable to provide teens with their own rooms. When Rusty turned 10, we moved our farm office out of our third bedroom so that he and Dottie could have their own rooms. While they still spend lots of time reading in the living space or playing outside with each other, they each like to have a space where they can keep their special things and do solitary activities like drawing (Dottie) or planning future backpacking trips (Rusty).

On a farm, teens whose homes don't allow them to have their own room can often still find privacy and time to be alone through being on the land. Corinne Hansch's three children all have their own rooms in their small house, but she said her kids also value the space on the farm. "There's 120 acres for them to go play on," Corinne said. Outbuildings can also be turned into spaces for teens to hang out on their own, even if they still sleep in a shared bedroom in the house.

At 18, Alijah Thorn already has many skills that he can use professionally, either on a farm or elsewhere.

HELPING TEENS LOOK TO THE FUTURE

Later in adolescence, teens begin the big (lifelong) work of discerning their purpose in the world and finding the work *they* want to do—which may or may not be farming. Even if they enjoy farming and the income that comes from helping with harvest, they may have other interests they want to pursue.

Kids raised on farms have watched the work up close their entire lives, so they usually already know the pros and the cons of farming. They also have more insight into what it means to work and earn an income than many kids who haven't grown up immersed in a family business. Bil Thorn and Kate Harwell observed that their 18-year-old son isn't rushing to leave home. "He knows how expensive life is," she said. "When we first moved here, it was really hard for us to get by." She said the prevailing wages in their community are very low. "We struggled a lot, and the farm pulled us up out of that struggle," she said. Her son enjoys learning about mechanics and works on all the farm vehicles: "He maintains our equipment, changes oil, works on them, and gets them going again." So even if he doesn't pursue farming specifically, he is developing skills he may use in his future professional life.

Corinne Hansch said that her kids "see how much work farming is and how much their mom and dad work. But they also see it's our income. They see cash coming in at market." She's not sure what her teens will want to pursue someday. But for now, the farm is a place where they can work, and there's room for them to someday become a bigger part of the farm business, if they want. "I'm keeping it open as a possibility," she said, "but I try to put zero pressure on them. Mostly I want them to find their true calling, passion, and joy."

DISCUSSION AND JOURNALING QUESTIONS

▶ *Take a moment to reflect on your own memories of being a tween/teen. What stands out as you remember your emotional state, your challenges, your growth, and the ways in which you were or weren't supported in becoming independent?*

▶ *If your children are tweens/teens now, what changes are you observing in them and in their relationship to the farm/homestead? How are you actively supporting them in developing maturity, responsibility, and independence?*

▶ *What is one additional responsibility you can add to your tween/teen's life right now? What is one additional form of independence you can offer them right now?*

Luna Argueta with her parents
La Finquita del Buho
Helvetia, Oregon

FARM KIDS
ALL
GROWN UP

RAISING KIDS ON A FARM or homestead is filled with challenges but also holds plenty of fun, laughter, and magic. The 18 or so years it takes to raise a child represent a big chunk of a parent or caregiver's life, but eventually kids grow up! So parenting is also about those future years, the ones when parents' influence will decrease. Like most parents, I hope the choices Casey and I make will help our children grow into responsible, happy adults. And, like most parents, I sometimes doubt our choices. We parents can do our best, but what will our children think and feel about being raised on a farm?

I can't time travel to talk to our own future grown-up children, but for this book I reached out to young adults who were raised on farms and homesteads to hear *their* thoughts about growing up in a farm or homestead setting and how those experiences shaped their lives. Much of what they reported confirmed both the joys and challenges that farm parents themselves recognize. These young adults are now able to look back and see how their childhoods shaped them for life. I found their accounts to be inspiring, hopeful, and universally filled with gratitude.

SARAH FINGER

Sarah Finger is a full-time artist living in Bellingham, Washington, the same community served by Cedarville Farm, the organic vegetable farm where she grew up. Cedarville Farm is where Casey and I first trained, and I had the privilege of knowing the farm and working alongside Sarah and her two siblings when they were still children. Already they had much to teach us! At 10, Sarah taught Casey that when you go to catch a chicken, you have to "*want* to catch the chicken," and her sister told us that when you bunch a head of leaf lettuce, you should hold it under your arm like you're holding a duck—which, of course, we'd never done. The Finger kids were my first introduction to the incredible competency of farm kids, and it was fun to connect again to hear Sarah's memories of growing up at Cedarville.

Sarah, now 28, has always felt pride in how her family has been integral in Whatcom County's local food scene. Her father helped start the now-thriving Bellingham Farmers Market decades ago and has employed and acted as mentor to many young farmers. But her biggest childhood memories are of having freedom and playing outside. For many years she and her siblings were homeschooled. Their days started with school in the mornings, and then her mom left to work off the farm and the kids had time to play outside all afternoon. "It was magical. The whole property was our extended playground," Sarah said. "That was so huge in my development and figuring out my independence."

Sarah recalled always doing chores around the house and then starting to help on the farm when she was very young. "I remember helping pack the CSA boxes and getting paid a quarter an hour as a kindergartner," she said, adding that it took a while for her work to be helpful but that she enjoyed it from the very beginning. "I had so much fun running around the packing station and doing small tasks like putting the squash in boxes."

Sarah Finger works in her home printmaking studio in Bellingham, Washington. Her family's farm inspired her to start her own small business.

Her contributions increased over time until she was working full-time as part of the crew in high school and during summers in college. Working alongside her dad's crew was a positive experience: "I got to form great relationships with these cool young adults I could look up to." Though she enjoyed working on the farm crew, Sarah never considered farming as a career path for herself. "Even though I loved working on the farm, I could see how much more work and responsibility went into actually running the business," Sarah said.

She also recognized some of the challenges for her family: "The farm was all-consuming for my dad, and it was hard for him to get away." Family vacations were often difficult to make happen. She was aware that some of her friends' families had more money, but also knew that "we ate the best food and had the strongest community, and our life felt so rich."

Sarah emphasized that her parents always gave their children a choice about how much to engage with the farm beyond their basic chores. "My parents were understanding. They recognized that I was a kid with kid interests and wanted to help me explore those interests."

When she went to college, she was amazed to meet peers who had never worked, and in some cases had parents who didn't *let* them work. "Having the importance of good, hard, honest work ingrained in me has done so much for me as an adult," Sarah said. Inspired by her father's entrepreneurship, she has been working as a full-time artist since 2020. "There are definitely strong ties between what I'm doing now and growing up on the farm, seeing my dad running his own business, forging his own path, and knowing that I could do the same with whatever my passion turned out to be."

ALANA KENAGY

Alana Kenagy, who uses they/them pronouns, has had many different relationships with their family's farm, Kenagy Family Farm in Hubbard, Oregon. While they were growing up, the farm grew fruit and vegetables for a local cannery and field crops such as wheat and crimson clover, and it had a pick-your-own strawberry patch. Since then, the farm has evolved and diversified, adding native seed crops and more, in part because of Alana's continued influence.

Alana, 34, grew up on the farm with their brother, parents, and grandparents and has fond memories of being with family and playing outside. They loved exploring along the Willamette River and building forts. As an adult, they realize that these experiences gave them a very different relationship with the natural world than what they see in their peers. "As I've gotten older, it's become even more apparent that I have a secure relationship with the earth," Alana said. "I trust the world. That benefits my mental, emotional, spiritual, and physical health."

Alana also started working on the farm at a young age. "That's where I learned math and customer service and adding in my head with the strawberry harvest," they said. Alana felt competent and physically strong as a child, which gave them confidence. "I got made fun of in school, but I was really strong," Alana said. "That contributed to my sense of self-security."

As Alana grew, their role in the farm grew, and in high school their parents asked both siblings to take a tractor safety course at the local community college to prepare them to operate machinery. Alana drove the combine and tillage tractor, and they remember getting the disc stuck in the tractor tire. "I was freaking out about how to fix that!" Alana remembered.

After graduating high school, Alana continued to work on the farm while exploring college coursework and eventually decided that they did want to work full-time with the family's operation—something their brother also does. However, after many years, they've stepped back, feeling frustrated by limits on their farm role. "I had the responsibilities of a boss and a manager and a regular employee," Alana said, "but I didn't have any of the decision-making control."

Alana Kenagy picks berries at their family's farm, just a short walk from their own home.

Alana lives a short walk from the farm and is still involved in several of the farm's enterprises while also operating a separate part-time business based out of a farm building. Alana sees their future still being somehow wrapped up in the future of the farm, and their life is still interconnected. "I walk on the farm multiple times a week and value getting to see things change," they said. "I value slowing down. I'm not just on the farm to get things done. I am just here to be with the land. And someday my stewardship may call me to be more involved and active again."

Alana sees many ways in which their farm upbringing shaped their values and choices as an adult. Among other things, they said, "I try to bring food with me wherever I go. I'm frequently ferrying extra produce, whether it's from the farm or from my friend's farm or from somebody else who had extra food. I bring it to people I love and people in need."

RAVEN BERMAN

Raven Berman, 29, grew up at his parents' remote homestead, 25 Mile Creek Farm, near Lake Chelan in the mountains of central Washington. Casey and I first met Raven when he was a kid running around barefoot as we helped his father, Jeff, put in a spring garden one year. Although they occasionally sold food off the farmstead, his parents grew food primarily for themselves, valuing their lifestyle on the land. "They get so much joy from seeing the entire life process of a plant that's going to provide food," Raven said.

Raven's sister was too much older to be a playmate, but two children his age lived next door. "I was outside all the time, running around. I knew the best trees to climb, the best undergrowth to go under and have a little fort. It was the ultimate way to grow up."

Raven's experience shifted when he started school and the neighboring children moved away. "Suddenly my life didn't revolve as much around being outside," he said. The family's land is more than 25 miles from the town of Chelan where he went to school. Raven's school bus ride was one of the longest in the state, averaging an hour each way. When he became more involved in sports and school, his family moved to town each winter to avoid the long and icy drive.

Having spent his early childhood on the farm, attending public middle school felt like a rough transition for Raven. His family's lifestyle was very different from that of many of his classmates. His father had built their house, and they used a composting outhouse toilet. "Using an outhouse was still normal to me until I started going to school," Raven said. "Then I'd have friends come visit or I'd talk about the outhouse and people said, 'What?' I realized maybe this is not normal for most people."

At first Raven found it hard to fit in with his peers in school, and that affected his relationship to the homestead. "I had this hippie kind of upbringing," he said. "It was like I had to be resistant to it almost because it was so counter to what all my friends were into." Although he did household chores, Raven didn't help much in the garden when he was a child. "I wasn't a very good worker, honestly, especially once I started being in school. I lost appreciation for the land, for the food I was eating, and for the responsibilities."

Raven Berman works remotely and spends one to two months at the farm every year helping his parents take care of their land. "I enjoy being there, and it's so rewarding doing the work."

Raven eventually found work that he enjoyed doing on the land. "I liked machine stuff." He helped with mowing, using the tiller, and splitting wood. His dad started offering to pay him to mow their large lawn, which led to Raven mowing their entire property and then mowing neighbors' properties as well. In addition, at age 14 he started working full-time at a Chelan resort every summer. "I developed a really deep understanding of work and money," he said.

Once Raven left for college, he said, his view of the farm changed. "Every year I develop deeper and deeper appreciation for being on the land, the upbringing I got, the value of eating healthy, good foods, and the whole life cycle of food," he said. Today Raven works as a wellness coach. "I want to encourage people to be active and eat well," he said. "That's how I grew up living."

In 2021, a wildfire burned large portions of Raven's family's land and destroyed one of their neighbor's houses. Raven's dad stayed up all night protecting their family's house, which caught on fire several times. "Those types of events make you appreciate everything even more," Raven said. "That was a pretty big wake-up call. Wow, this is a special place."

LUNA AND JACOB ARGUETA

Luna and Jacob Argueta grew up with their brother at La Finquita del Buho, a small mixed vegetable and flower farm on the outskirts of Hillsboro, Oregon. During their childhood, their father stayed home as the primary parent; this allowed him to also be a full-time farmer, as he still is today. Their mother worked as a doctor and medical director, but she put in long hours on the farm in the evenings and weekends. Since Luna, 22, and Jacob, 28, were children, the farm has offered CSA shares, sold at market, and raised animals for personal use and sales.

I was able to connect with both Jacob (the oldest sibling), Luna (the youngest sibling), and their mom, Lyn Jacobs, about their experiences

Luna and her parents feed their goats cottonwood branches. Luna continues to live and help on the farm.

with being a farm family. Not surprisingly, the grown children led with their love of being outside as kids. "When I was younger, I remember the farm seemed huge, even though it was just two and a half acres," Jacob said. "The orchard, the conifer stand, the barn, the grapevines, and the enormous walnut tree were all their own worlds." Luna remembers being barefoot and running laps around her mom while she transplanted out in the field. "She was there watching me, but I was just running around doing my own thing." Luna loved the freedom she felt.

Because Lyn worked during the week, the family's main harvest day was Sunday, and from a young age, the kids were expected to help as much as they could. Both Luna and Jacob admitted that it took time for them to enjoy helping in this way. "I remember when I was really young faking being sick so I didn't have to go help harvest the vegetables," Luna said. Jacob said that expectations grew as they got older, and they helped with many tasks around the farm and home: clearing weeds, stacking hay and animal feed, splitting firewood, moving animals, helping with market chores, and more. Jacob said, "We often made the work fun—for us at least—by teasing and competing with each other."

Luna Argueta's father, Juvencio, drives the sheep and goats in for the night.

Both Luna and Jacob said they enjoyed the work more as they grew older, and Luna especially became an integral part of the farm crew in high school. She took a lead in helping to coordinate the harvest, which she continues to do.

Jacob's appreciation of farm life was tested when he was a young teenager because he was frustrated by the poor internet access at the farm and some of the differences he perceived between his life and that of his peers. "I was jealous of friends who could eat junk food regularly," he said. "I didn't appreciate the fresh produce and home cooking then." Luna really valued the food they ate growing up. "I don't remember ever not liking vegetables," she said. "I went away on trips and missed vegetables."

One of Luna's favorite parts about growing up on the farm was working with their goats. She especially remembers taking care of a small runt goat with selenium deficiency that everyone thought could not survive. "I spent so much time feeding this little goat. His legs straightened out, and he was able to walk eventually," she said. "He was the sweetest goat ever. He followed me around the farm."

Luna lives in her own small cabin on the farm. While she is currently working full-time as an aide at a medical clinic, she sees the family's farm as being an important part of her future. When we spoke, she was about to start an organic agriculture postgraduate certification program to learn new ideas to implement on the farm someday. "I'm trying to get outside knowledge and then be able to eventually take over the farm and put new systems in place," she said.

Jacob's path has taken him far from the farm to his current work as a research technician for the University of Alaska, but those values and lessons are part of his life. "Growing up on a farm set the precedent early that I wanted an active job where I was outside a lot," he said. "It helped instill in me the values of self-sufficiency, hard work, sense of place, and community."

DISCUSSION AND JOURNALING QUESTIONS

▶ *When you imagine your children as adults, how do you hope they will remember their life on your farm or homestead?*

▶ *What are the values and skills you want your children to take into adulthood? How are you currently teaching or modeling these values or skills?*

▶ *How important is it to you that your children stay involved with your farm or farming? What are you doing to help make farming or homesteading a positive option for them?*

▶ *How will you feel if your children pursue other goals? How will you support them?*

AFTERWORD

Reader, thank you for joining me on this book's journey. Wherever you are on your own farming and parenting journey, I hope you found ideas, inspiration, and comfort in these pages. As I talked with other farmers, reflected on our family's own experiences, and wrote these words, a few themes stood out that I want to highlight in closing.

Connect with others; ask for help. Time and time again, as I heard farmers' stories of success and challenges, people shared the ways they needed help from others as they navigated parenting. Some people found farms and land to be perfect places to live in a community setting, where more adults could help with the children, whether that was sharing a large house on a double lot in town or sharing a large property with other families or extended family.

But support can come in many forms: from partners and co-parents, the farm community (employees, coworkers, employers, and customers), childcare providers, extended family, neighbors, friends, and even older children. If you need help, ask for help. Build networks of people who can help support you, your family, your child, and your farm through what are likely to be tumultuous times.

Families and farmers need support systems. Beyond immediate circles of relationships, farmers thrive when there are also larger systems to support them and their families. Farmers who live in communities, regions, and countries with such support overall reported less stress than those who lived in areas with less support. Farmers who had better access to quality affordable childcare, quality affordable health care, and paid parental leave found that the adjustment to parenting felt less like a crisis for their farm. In 2023, the American Farm Bureau and the National Farmers Union included childcare in their policy priorities for the federal farm bill, so perhaps more farming communities will see these kinds of systemic supports in coming years.

Parenting starts out being incredibly hard but eventually gets easier. And, of course, if you read these chapters in sequential order, I'm sure you noticed the beautiful trajectory of children growing from helpless babies into competent tweens, teens, and eventually adults. When you are awake in the night with a teething baby, wondering how in the world you will get through the next day's big harvest, it's hard to imagine that someday that baby will be not only sleeping through the night but perhaps also helping you in the fields.

Yes, those first years require enormous sacrifices and commitment, but they really do pass. Sharing a farm and home with our 10- and 13-year-old feels more like being with two other adults as they increasingly grow capable of taking initiative and completing essential household and farm tasks with less guidance. They are kind, funny, imaginative, and delightful to be around.

I will miss our children's daily help and company when they are old enough and ready to move on to their own adventures, which feels like it is coming all too soon.

FEATURED FAMILIES AND FARMS

Thank you again to all the farmers (and grown farm kids!) who shared their experiences with me for this book. If you'd like to learn more about their farms and see the diversity of voices represented, here is a bit more info.

Lyn Jacobs and Luna and Jacob Argueta (grown farm kids)
La Finquita del Buho, Helvetia, Oregon

Land base: 3 acres
Crops: Vegetables, flowers, meat
Family dynamic: 2 parents, 3 grown children
Website: finquita.com
Instagram: @la_finquita_del_buho

Raven Berman (grown farm kid)
25 Mile Creek Farm, Chelan, Washington

Land base: 10 acres
Crops: Mixed vegetables and fruit
Family dynamic: 2 parents, 2 grown children

The Arqueta Family

Emily Board and Dan Brisebois
Tourne-Sol Cooperative Farm, Les Cèdres, Quebec, Canada

Land base: 17 acres
Crops: Mixed vegetable CSA and seed company
Family dynamic: 2 parents, 3 children (ages 1 to 10)
Farm dynamic: 10 owners and multiple households
Website: fermetournesol.qc.ca
Instagram: @fermetournesol

Elise Bortz
Elysian Fields Farm, Cedar Grove, North Carolina

Land base: 40 acres
Crops: Vegetables
Family dynamic: 2 parents, 2 children (ages 6 and 8)
Website: elysianfarm.com
Instagram: @elysianfieldsfarm

Brooke Bridges
Soul Fire Farm, Grafton, New York

Land base: 80 acres
Crops: Fruits, plant medicine, pasture-raised livestock, honey, mushrooms, vegetables
Family dynamic: 2 parents, 2 children (ages 2 months and 19 months)
Farm dynamic: Large team with multiple households living on farm
Website: soulfirefarm.org
Instagram: @soulfirefarm

Kristen Pool Cohen and her children

Jacob Slosberg and Amy Frye

Tara Chapman

Two Hives Honey, Manor, Texas

Land base: 5.5 acres
Crops and Services: Honey, beekeeping education
Family dynamic: 2 parents, 1 child (age 1)
Website: twohiveshoney.com
Instagram: @twohives

Kristin Pool Cohen

Super House, Portland, Oregon

Land base: Double town lot
Crops: Vegetables, fruit
Family dynamic: 2 households sharing 1 house (2 parents and 2 kids each)
Website: kristinpool.com
Instagram: @kpoolproductions

Sarah Finger (grown farm kid)

Cedarville Farm, Bellingham, Washington

Land base: 8.5 acres
Crops: Vegetables, herbs, CSA
Family dynamic: 2 parents, 3 grown children

Amy Frye

Boldly Grown Farm, Bow, Washington

Land base: 58 acres
Crops: Vegetables
Family dynamic: 2 parents, 2 children (ages 3 and 6)
Website: boldlygrownfarm.com
Instagram: @boldlygrownfarm

Jordan Goldsmith

Moonrose Farm, Rehoboth, Massachusetts

Land base: 7 acres
Crops: Vegetables, flowers, eggs, bread
Family dynamic: 2 parents, 1 child (age 1)
Website: moonrosefarm.com
Instagram: @moonrosefarm

Corinne Hansch

Lovin' Mama Farm, Amsterdam, New York

Land base: 120 acres
Crops: Vegetables, herbs, flowers
Family dynamic: 2 parents, 3 children (ages 10, 15, and 16)
Website: lovinmamafarm.com
Instagram: @lovinmamafarm

Alana Kenagy

Alana Kenagy (grown farm kid)
Kenagy Family Farm, Hubbard, Oregon

Land base: 450 acres
Crops: Seed crops, vegetables, grains
Family dynamic: 2 parents, 2 grown
  children, extended family
Website: kenagyfamilyfarm.com

Sarah Kostyu
K7 Farm, Concord, Michigan

Land base: 15 acres
Crops: Vegetables, fruit, meat, eggs, dairy
Family dynamic: 2 parents, 10 children
  (ages 3 months to 19 years)
Website: k7farm.com
Instagram: @k7_farm

Alyson Larkin
Wingspan Farm, McMinnville, Oregon

Land base: 123 acres
Crops: Vegetables, fruit, eggs, meat
Family dynamic: 2 parents, 3 children
  (ages 4, 11, and 15)
Farm dynamic: 3 households sharing farm

The Larkin Family

John McCafferty
Pleasant River Produce, Otago, New Zealand

Land base: 30 acres
Crops: Vegetables
Family dynamic: 2 parents, 3 children
  (ages 1, 3, and 11)
Instagram: @pleasant_river_produce

Katrina McQuail
Meeting Place Organic Farm, Lucknow,
Ontario, Canada

Land base: 100 acres
Crops: Meat, eggs, vegetables, apples,
  seedlings
Family dynamic: 2 parents, 3 children
  (infant; ages 2 and 4), grandparents
Website: meetingplaceorganicfarm.ca
Instagram: @meetingplaceorganicfarm

Christina Menchini

Campfire Farms, Mulino, Oregon

Land base: 30 acres
Crops: Pork, chicken
Family dynamic: 2 parents, 2 children
  (ages 3 and 6)
Website: campfirefarms.com
Instagram: @campfirefarms

Benina Montes

Burroughs Family Farms, Denair, California

Land base: 1,400 acres
Crops: Almonds, olives, meat, eggs
Family dynamic: 2 parents, 4 children
  (ages 6, 8, 10, and 12), extended family
Website: burroughsfamilyfarms.com
Instagram: @burroughs.family.farms

Hanako Myers and Marko Colby

Midori Farm, Quilcene, Washington

Land base: 29 acres
Crops: Vegetables, seedlings, seeds,
  fermented vegetables
Family dynamic: 2 parents, 1 child (age 2)
Website: midori-farm.com
Instagram: @midorifarmer2007

Sara and Symbria Patterson

Red Acre Farm CSA, Cedar City, Utah

Land base: 2 acres
Crops: Full-diet CSA
Family dynamic: 1 grown child, 1 parent
Website: redacrefarmcsa.org
Instagram: @redacrefarm

Daisy Remington

Auckland, New Zealand

Land base: 10 acres
Crops: Vegetables, fruit, meat, eggs
Family dynamic: 2 parents, 2 children
  (ages 9 and 14)
Website: apocketfullofhay.com
Instagram: @apocketfullofhay

Daisy Remington

Diane Saleh

Halal Pastures, Rock Tavern, New York

Land base: 14 acres
Crops: Vegetables, meat
Family dynamic: 2 parents, 3 children
  (ages 3, 4, and 10)
Website: halalpastures.com
Instagram: @halalpasturesfarms

Tory Shelley

Featherbed Lane Farm, Ballston Spa,
New York

Land base: 63 acres
Crops: Mixed vegetable CSA
Family dynamic: 1 parent, 1 child (age 2)
Website: featherbedlanefarm.com
Instagram: @featherbed_lane_farm_csa

Bil Thorn and Kate Harwell

Sky Island Farm, Humptulips, Washington

Land base: 15 acres
Crops: Vegetables, fruit, herbs, flowers
Family dynamic: 2 parents, 2 children
  (ages 16 and 18)
Website: skyislandfarmcsa.com
Instagram: @skyislandfarm

SUGGESTED READING AND OTHER RESOURCES

BOOKS

These wonderful books go deeper into many of the topics addressed by this book, including more ideas for seasonal outdoor activities for the whole family. See also the list of seasonal picture books on pages 57–59.

A Little Bit of Dirt: 55+ Science and Art Activities to Reconnect Children with Nature, Asia Citro, The Innovation Press, 2016.

And Baby Makes Three: The Six-Step Plan for Preserving Marital Intimacy and Rekindling Romance After Baby Arrives, John Gottman, PhD, and Julie Schwartz Gottman, PhD, Harmony, 2008.

Family Homesteading: The Ultimate Guide to Self-Sufficiency for the Whole Family, Teri Page, Skyhorse Publishing, 2018.

Foraging with Kids: 52 Wild and Free Edibles to Enjoy with Your Children, Adele Nozedar, Nourish, 2018.

Gardening with Children: Brooklyn Botanic Garden Guides for a Greener Planet, Monika Hanneman and more, Brooklyn Botanic Garden, 2011.

Grow Wild: The Whole-Child, Whole-Family, Nature-Rich Guide to Moving More, Katy Bowman, Propriometrics Press, 2021.

Heaven on Earth: A Handbook for Parents of Young Children, Sharifa Oppenheimer, SteinerBooks, 2006.

Herbal Adventures: Backyard Excursions and Kitchen Creations for Kids and Their Families, Rachel Jepson Wolf, Young Voyageur, 2018.

How to Raise an Adult: Break Free of the Overparenting Trap and Prepare Your Kid for Success, Julie Lythcott-Haims, St. Martin's Griffin, 2016.

Jim Trelease's Read-Aloud Handbook: Eighth Edition, Jim Trelease, edited by Cyndi Giorgis, Penguin Books, 2019.

Last Child in the Woods: Saving Our Children from Nature-Deficit Disorder, Richard Louv, Algonquin Books, 2008.

Nature Play at Home: Creating Outdoor Spaces That Connect Children with the Natural World, Nancy Striniste, Timber Press, 2019.

Simplicity Parenting: Using the Extraordinary Power of Less to Raise Calmer, Happier, and More Secure Kids, Kim John Payne with Lisa M. Ross, Ballantine Books, 2010.

Taking Charge of Your Fertility, 20th Anniversary Edition: The Definitive Guide to Natural Birth Control, Pregnancy Achievement, and Reproductive Health, Toni Weschler, William Morrow Paperbacks, 2015.

The Artful Year: Celebrating the Seasons & Holidays with Crafts & Recipes, Jean Van't Hul, Roost Books, 2015.

The Encyclopedia of Country Living, 50th Anniversary Edition: The Original Manual for Living off the Land & Doing It Yourself, Carla Emery, Sasquatch Books, 2019.

We Garden Together!: Projects for Kids: Learn, Grow, and Connect with Nature, Jane Hirschi and Educators at City Sprouts, Storey Publishing, 2023.

OTHER RESOURCES

Carrying Matters
https://carryingmatters.co.uk
Dr. Rosie Knowles's website, Carrying Matters, offers guidance and tutorials for safe use of slings and other baby carriers. It also features articles and information about baby carrying benefits.

Cultivate Safety
https://cultivatesafety.org
Run by the National Children's Center for Rural and Agricultural Health and Safety (NCCRAHS) and the National Farm Medicine Center, this website provides information and resources about keeping kids safe while living, working, or playing on farms.

Department of Labor's Youth Labor Agricultural Employment
https://dol.gov/general/topic /youthlabor/agriculturalemployment
The US Department of Labor provides this website as a resource for learning about federal and state-specific laws for children doing agricultural work.

Farm Aid Farmer Hotline
https://farmaid.org/our-work /resources-for-farmers
1-800-FARM-AID
Farm Aid offers farmers multiple ways to connect and ask for help via their website or their hotline. Farm Aid's trained hotline operators guide farmers to specific resources for their needs.

National Agricultural Law Center
https://nationalaglawcenter.org /child-labor-laws
The National Agricultural Law Center has an article on their website summarizing child labor laws in the United States.

Western Regional Agricultural Stress Assistance Program
https://farmstress.us
The Western Regional Agricultural Stress Assistance Program provides information and resources for identifying and addressing farm-specific stress.

ACKNOWLEDGMENTS

Books grow from many sources! I am filled with immense gratitude for all the people who helped me cultivate this one. Thank you to:

Our land, which has fed and nourished our family and community for almost two decades. The land where we live and farm was once stolen by force from the Kalapuya, whose descendants comprise part of the Confederated Tribes of Grand Ronde Community of Oregon and still live in our community and share their stories and knowledge about this place.

All the farmers and families who reached out to me and shared their stories and experiences. There are more than I could begin to include, but each one informed me as I wrote. This book literally couldn't exist without your support, honesty, and enthusiasm for the project and the goal of helping other farm families thrive.

All our Oakhill Organics customers and employees—our wider farm family! Casey and I couldn't have farmed without you, and your generosity and encouragement through our early years of parenting helped us through some very challenging times.

Our farmer friends and peers who have shared invaluable knowledge with us as we have learned and grown during our farming journey—and especially the amazing crew from the annual Northwest Farmer-to-Farmer Exchange gatherings at Breitenbush Hot Springs, where I had my very first conversations with other farmers about the challenges of balancing our work with parenting.

Growing for Market magazine editor Andrew Mefferd, for recognizing the value of talking about how our personal lives overlap with our professional lives as farmers.

Lynn Byczynski, *Growing for Market*'s founder, for being the first to give my farm writing a publishing home, supporting my writing over many years, and writing the beautiful foreword for this book.

Kirstin Shockey, for your encouragement and guidance during the mysterious first steps of publishing and for the introduction to Storey.

Everyone at Storey, for seeing the value of this topic and working with me to create an awesome book. Especially to Carleen Madigan, for helping me shape this book from the beginning, and Lisa Hiley, Erin Dawson, Nancy Ringer, and Alissa Faden, for helping me magically transform my manuscript into a real book.

The talented Shawn Linehan and so many other photographers, for providing beautiful images to bring these stories vibrantly to life.

Shoshanah Inwood, Florence Becot, and Rachel Van Boven, for all the work you are doing to help farmers and farm families thrive.

Sylla McClellan of Third Street Books in McMinnville, Oregon, for being our farm's fairy godmother and a steadfast promoter of community, local businesses, good food, writers, and books.

All my friends who listened to my frustrations and helped celebrate my successes in this and many endeavors, especially Aynsley, Bethany, Rebecca, Leslie, Angela, Julie, Rosemary, Sonja, Sarah, and Kate. Trying to do any kind of work—farming, writing, or otherwise—while being a mom is tough, and you all have helped me navigate that journey.

My parents, who always believed in my dreams and goals. When I was double majoring in English and art during college, my mom always told people that someday I'd write and illustrate books. Look, Mom, I'm doing it! Also, for being the most amazing Mimi and Pops to my kids. Your daily presence in our lives is a gift.

Finally, to the three people who made me a parent and who walk every day with me: Casey, Rusty, and Dottie. Thank you for more joy and love than I can ever put into words.

INDEX

Page numbers in *italics* indicate photos.

P

streamlining farming operations, 178–79
stress
    reduction, 97–111
    signs of, 106–8
    support systems for, 217
supervision of children, 33–36. *See also* childcare
support
    forms of, 216–17
    for homeschooling, 92, 94–95
    for new parents, 137–38
    systems of, 217

T

teens
    chores for, 79
    needs of, 191–203
Thomas, Kai, 140
Thorn, Alijah, 201
Thorn, Arianna, 62, 75
Thorn, Bil, 24, *24*, 74, 102, *102*, 184, 188–89, 193, 221
time off, scheduling, 104
time requirements for homeschooling, 89–90
toddlers
    chores for, 77
    toys, 40–41
transitioning to farm life, ages of children and, 188–89
tweens
    chores for, 78–79
    needs of, 191–203

U

unstructured play, 37–38, 40–42

V

vacations, 104
Van Boven, Rachel, 108–9

W

washing up outdoors, 44
water play, 40
work, 63–81, 66
    benefits of, 64–65, 196–97
    beyond the farm, 197–98
    dangerous for children, 158
    ethic, building, 26–27, 70–73
    homeschooling and, 86
    as a learning experience, 86
    legal issues, 67
    paid, 73–74, 76
    parties, 54
    physical movement and, 197
    during pregnancy, 128–36
    shared between two partners, 160–61
    stages of children's participation in, 66–79
    teen labor and, 196